Democracy on the Edge

Navigating Loyalty, Truth, and Power in Turbulent Times

Maggie White

"Society in Debate™:
Perspectives on Key Issues" series, vol. 5

Title: Democracy on the Edge: Navigating Loyalty, Truth, and Power in Turbulent Times

Author: Maggie White

Series: Society in Debate: Perspectives on Key Issues, vol. 5

First Edition: 2024

ISBN : 9798874191177

Contents

"A genuine leader is not a searcher for consensus but a molder of consensus." – Martin Luther King Jr.

Introduction

In a time when the fabric of democracy seems increasingly strained, this book offers an unflinching gaze into the heart of modern democratic struggles. As we embark on this exploration, it is striking to note that only 22% of Americans believe that political leaders face consequences for acting unethically, revealing a deep-seated cynicism about the integrity of the political system[1]. This sentiment is echoed in the widespread view of the political landscape as "divisive" and "polarized", with terms like "corrupt", "messy", "chaos", "broken", and "dysfunctional" frequently surfacing in discussions about politics[2].

Such a landscape is fertile ground for the discourse presented here. This book delves into the intricate dance of political loyalty versus constitutional duty, threading through the complicated tapestry of progressive and conservative viewpoints. It scrutinizes the role of the media in crafting political narratives, addressing the pervasive concerns over media bias and misinformation, and reflects on the legitimacy of election outcomes and the balance of power between executive and legislative branches.

The book's approach is grounded in a reality where 65% of adults feel exhausted and 55% feel angry when thinking about politics, reflecting a climate of emotional fatigue and frustration that permeates political engagement. These figures underscore the urgency and relevance of the topics discussed in this book.

This book is not just an academic analysis; it is a mirror reflecting the troubled waters of contemporary democracy. It draws from a society where only 9% of adults feel hopeful and a mere 4% feel excited about politics, painting a sobering picture of the current political sentiment. This book serves as a guide through these

---

[1] https://www.pewresearch.org/politics/2023/09/19/the-biggest-problems-and-greatest-strengths-of-the-u-s-political-system/
[2] https://www.pewresearch.org/politics/2023/09/19/americans-feelings-about-politics-polarization-and-the-tone-of-political-discourse/

tumultuous times, providing insights and understanding essential for anyone interested in the future of democracy.

As we navigate through these pages, we find ourselves not only dissecting the anatomy of democratic systems but also confronting the very essence of what it means to be a part of a democratic society. "Democracy on the Edge" is an essential read for those who seek to understand the complexities and challenges that define democracy today, and for those who aspire to be part of shaping its tomorrow.

Note to the reader: Embracing the Nuances and Complexity of Democracy and Political Ethics Debates

As you embark on this journey through "Democracy on the Edge: Navigating Loyalty, Truth, and Power in Turbulent Times," you may notice that some subjects and themes within the book bear a close resemblance to each other. This similarity is not coincidental but is a fundamental aspect of the book's design. The overlapping and interrelated nature of these subjects exemplifies the intricate and multifaceted character of the issues surrounding democracy, political ethics, and leadership.

Each chapter, while appearing similar in context, explores unique nuances and perspectives of these broad themes. This approach is essential for a comprehensive understanding of the topics. It allows us to dissect each theme layer by layer, revealing the complex interplay of historical, cultural, political, and technological factors that shape our perspectives on these vital issues.

For example, the chapters on "The Ethics of Political Loyalty vs. Constitutional Duty" and "The Accountability of Political Leaders in Democratic Societies" both deal with aspects of political ethics, yet each tackles different dimensions – one focuses on the conflict between loyalty and duty, and the other on the broader implications of political accountability. Similarly, "Media's Role in Shaping Political Narratives" and "The Influence of Social Media on Political Mobilization and Radicalization" both examine the media's impact but from distinct angles, one through traditional media's lens and the other through the evolving realm of social media.

This structured overlap is crucial in unraveling the layers of each debate, allowing for an exploration of every facet and viewpoint. It is through this comprehensive examination that we can truly appreciate the depth and scope of the issues at hand. This deep dive into multiple aspects of similar themes ensures an exhaustive exploration of each subject, leaving no stone unturned in our quest to understand the complexities of modern democracy and its challenges.

As you navigate through the chapters, I invite you to embrace both the subtle differences and the apparent similarities. They are the threads that weave together the rich tapestry of discussions in this book, offering a fuller, more nuanced understanding of the issues that shape our political and ethical landscape.

Chapter 1: The Ethics of Political Loyalty vs. Constitutional Duty

Debating whether elected officials should prioritize party loyalty or constitutional principles.

The heart of the debate on the ethics of political loyalty versus constitutional duty centers around the conflict between the immediate, tangible demands of party allegiance and the more abstract, yet foundational, obligations to constitutional principles. This tension becomes the focal point of contention because it strikes at the core of what it means to be an elected official in a democratic system.

On one side of the debate, there's the argument that political loyalty is essential for maintaining party unity and effectiveness. Proponents of this view argue that, in a practical sense, adherence to party lines ensures that policies are pushed forward efficiently and that the party's agenda is advanced. They posit that without such loyalty, the party could become fractured, leading to political instability and an inability to govern effectively.

Conversely, the other side of the debate champions the primacy of constitutional duty. Advocates of this perspective argue that the constitution represents the fundamental law of the land, embodying the principles and values upon which the nation is founded. They assert that elected officials, having sworn an oath to the constitution, must prioritize these enduring principles over transient party goals. This viewpoint stresses that allegiance to the constitution safeguards democracy, protects minority rights, and ensures a check on the powers of the government.

The crux of this debate lies in its implications for democratic governance and the role of elected officials. The polarizing aspect is not just a choice between two paths, but a question of identity and purpose: Should elected officials see themselves primarily as representatives of their party or as guardians of the constitution? This question provokes strong debate because it challenges fundamental beliefs about the nature of democracy, the role of representation, and the meaning of accountability. It forces a reexamination of the balance between collective responsibility to a political group and individual responsibility to a broader, more abstract set of principles. This clash of ideals is what makes the topic so contentious and so critical in discussions about democratic governance and ethics in politics.

Progressive and Conservative Viewpoints:

Identifying the Progressive Viewpoint

Aspect: Prioritization of Constitutional Duty

Justification: The aspect of prioritizing constitutional duty over party loyalty can be seen as aligning with progressive viewpoints. This stance typically emphasizes the need for adherence to principles that reflect modern interpretations of constitutional values, often advocating for social reform and the protection of individual rights. Progressives may argue that the constitution, while a historical document, is a living framework meant to evolve with societal changes. Therefore, they often emphasize the importance of interpreting the constitution in a way that addresses contemporary issues and promotes equality and justice. This approach to constitutional duty reflects a progressive inclination towards change, adaptation, and the pursuit of social equity.

Identifying the Conservative Viewpoint:

Aspect: Emphasis on Political Loyalty

Justification: The argument favoring political loyalty aligns with conservative viewpoints. Conservatives often value the preservation of established norms and traditions, which in this context translates to maintaining party cohesion and unity. They may view party loyalty as a means to uphold and continue traditional policies and principles that the party represents. This perspective emphasizes stability, continuity, and respect for the established political order. Conservatives might argue that party loyalty is crucial for effective governance and upholding the values and agendas that their constituents support. This view reflects conservative traits such as valuing historical context, resisting rapid change, and focusing on maintaining established systems and traditions within the political landscape.

Political Analysis

Progressive/Liberal (Left) Viewpoints:

In Support of Prioritizing Constitutional Duty: A significant portion of the left likely views prioritizing constitutional duty positively. This segment, which may constitute around 70%, aligns with progressive ideals of change, modern interpretations of the constitution, and social reform. They might argue that the constitution should be a living document, adapting to new societal challenges and protecting individual rights.

In Support of Political Loyalty: There might be a smaller segment within the left, estimated at 30%, that supports the idea of political loyalty. This group might argue that in certain circumstances, party unity is crucial for the effective implementation of progressive policies and for countering conservative agendas.

Conservative/Republican (Right) Viewpoints:

In Support of Prioritizing Constitutional Duty: A minority within the conservative camp, possibly around 20%, might support prioritizing constitutional duty. This group could argue that the constitution's original intent and principles should guide political decisions, even if it occasionally conflicts with party lines.

In Support of Political Loyalty: The majority of the right, estimated at 80%, likely advocates for political loyalty. This perspective aligns with conservative values of tradition, stability, and upholding established party principles. They might believe that party loyalty is essential for maintaining political order and ensuring the implementation of their policy agendas.

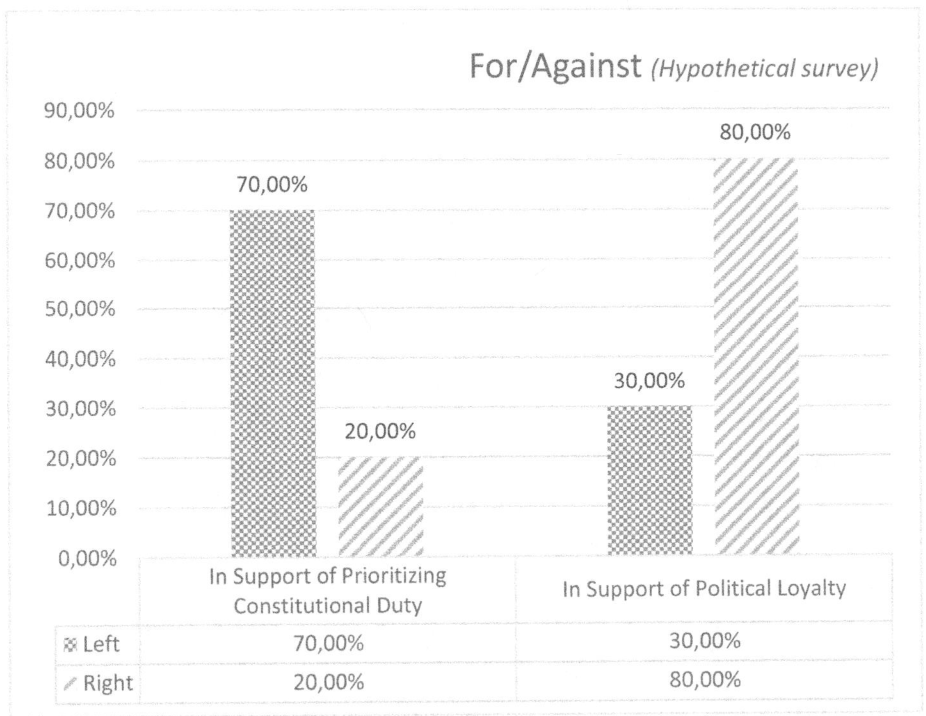

	In Support of Prioritizing Constitutional Duty	In Support of Political Loyalty
Left	70,00%	30,00%
Right	20,00%	80,00%

To Know

Partisan Fighting as a Key Issue: A significant 86% of Americans believe that Republicans and Democrats are more focused on fighting each other than on solving problems. This statistic highlights the pervasive issue of partisan conflict in American politics, which is directly relevant to the debate on whether elected officials should prioritize party loyalty or constitutional principles.[3]

---

[3] https://www.pewresearch.org/politics/2023/09/19/the-biggest-problems-and-greatest-strengths-of-the-u-s-political-system/

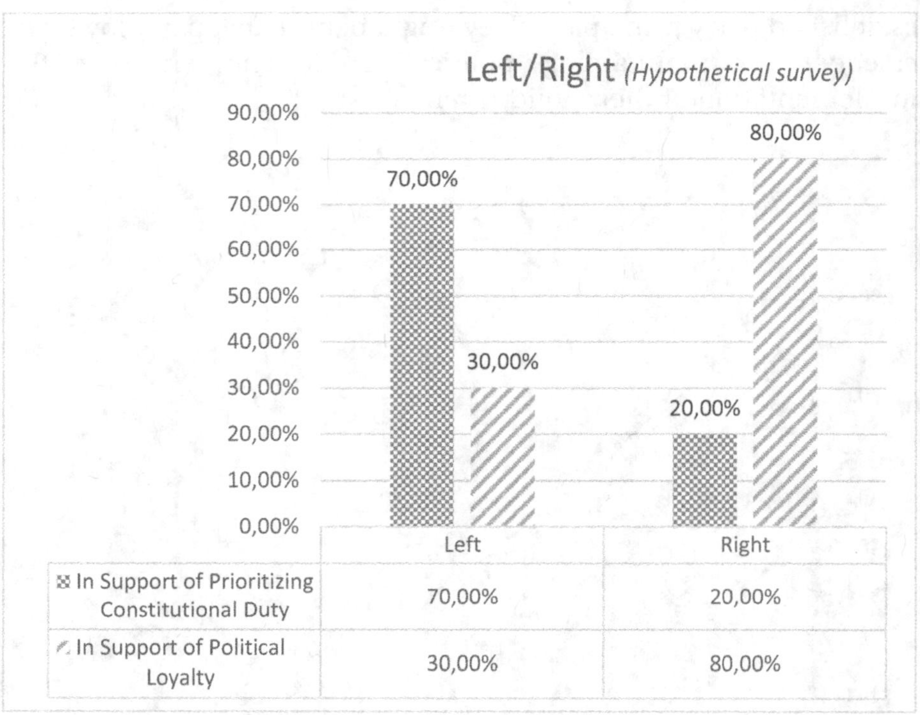

	Left	Right
In Support of Prioritizing Constitutional Duty	70,00%	20,00%
In Support of Political Loyalty	30,00%	80,00%

Motions of the debate

Coalition's Motion (Progressive Viewpoint):

"This house supports the prioritization of constitutional duty over party loyalty in governance, advocating that elected officials should foremost uphold constitutional principles and values, even when they conflict with party agendas."

Opposition's Motion (Conservative Viewpoint):

"This house opposes the prioritization of constitutional duty over party loyalty, asserting that elected officials should primarily uphold the agenda and unity of their party, as it represents the mandate given by their electorate."

Coalition Speech

Ladies and gentlemen, esteemed members of this house, today we stand at a crossroads in our understanding of governance and the role of those who steer the ship of state. I rise to affirm that the guiding star for our elected officials must be their constitutional duty, a beacon that shines brighter than the flickering candle of party loyalty.

Imagine a nation where the constitution is not just a document, but the soul of its democracy. It's a shield that guards democratic values and the rights of the minority. Remember the times when adherence to the constitution thwarted the rise of authoritarianism. Think of the times when nations, guided by their constitutions, stood resilient in the face of turmoil. This is the power of constitutional duty – it is not just a legal obligation, but the very essence of a functioning democracy.

Now, consider the role of an elected official. They are not just representatives of a party; they are guardians of the whole populace. How often have we seen the pitfalls when leaders choose party over people? The public disenfranchisement, the trust eroded. By prioritizing constitutional duty, these officials honor their oath to serve every citizen, not just those who share their party banner.

But let's also talk about stability and governance. The constitution is a stabilizing force, a checks and balances system that prevents extreme, unbalanced policies. History has shown us that when constitutional guidance is the compass, political stability follows. On the other hand, short-term party agendas can undermine long-term national interests. We've seen policies enacted in haste, for party gain, only to be reversed at great cost.

And finally, let's discuss ethics and public trust. Upholding the constitution is the cornerstone of ethical governance. It's about integrity, about doing what is right, not what is easy. Remember the leaders who are revered not because they followed the party line, but because they stood by their constitutional obligations. It's their legacy that lights our way.

Public trust – this is what we risk when we prioritize party over principle. Surveys have shown that when governments put constitutional values first, public trust is higher. People believe in a system that upholds the constitution as its guiding principle.

So, I ask you, which path should we choose? One that leads to a democracy where the constitution is our guide, our protector, and our promise to every citizen? Or one where party loyalty trumps the very principles upon which our nations are built?

Ladies and gentlemen, as we stand at this crossroads, I urge you to choose the path of constitutional duty. It is the path of democracy, stability, ethics, and trust. This house must support the prioritization of constitutional duty over party loyalty, for in doing so, we uphold the very essence of what it means to serve the people.

Thank you.

Summary of the coalition's arguments

I. Upholding Democratic Principles and Values
A. Constitutional duty as a safeguard for democracy
- Constitutions are designed to protect democratic values and minority rights.
- Historical examples where constitutional adherence prevented authoritarianism.
B. Elected officials' accountability to all citizens, not just their party
- Representatives serve the entire populace, not just those who voted for them.
- Case studies where prioritizing party over constitution led to public disenfranchisement.
II. Ensuring Long-Term Stability and Governance
A. The constitution as a stabilizing force in politics
- The constitution provides checks and balances that prevent extreme policies.
- Instances where constitutional guidance led to long-term political stability.
B. The danger of short-term party agendas
- Short-term party goals can undermine long-term national interests.
- Examples where party loyalty led to policies that were later reversed or caused harm.
III. Promoting Ethical Governance and Public Trust
A. Constitutional duty as an ethical cornerstone for elected officials

- Upholding the constitution fosters integrity and ethical governance.
- Historical figures revered for prioritizing constitutional duty over party loyalty.
B. Maintaining public trust in government institutions
- Public trust is higher in governments that prioritize constitutional values.
- Surveys showing public disillusionment when party loyalty overrides constitutional duty.

Opposition Speech

Ladies and gentlemen, esteemed members of this august house, today I stand before you to shed light on a fundamental truth often overshadowed in the discourse of governance. The proposition today suggests that constitutional duty should supersede party loyalty, but I submit to you that this is a narrow view, one that overlooks the very fabric of our democratic system.

Let us begin by understanding the essence of effective governance. It is unity, not division, that propels a nation forward. Consider the efficiency and decisiveness that party loyalty brings to the legislative process. History is replete with examples where party unity has enabled swift and effective policy implementation. Contrast this with governments crippled by internal strife, where conflicting loyalties lead to stalemate and dysfunction. Party loyalty is not a hindrance, but a catalyst for action.

Now, let us turn to the representation of the electorate's mandate. When people cast their votes, they endorse not just individuals, but platforms and ideologies. The electorate expects their representatives to adhere to these promises. Straying from party lines is not just a breach of loyalty; it is a betrayal of the voters' trust. Consider the consequences when politicians disregard their party's stance. It leads to a loss of faith, a feeling of disenchantment among those who trusted them to bring their collective vision to life.

Moreover, we must acknowledge the importance of preserving political ideologies and long-term goals. Party loyalty ensures the continuity and consistency of these ideologies. It allows for the fulfillment of long-term strategic plans that are essential for a nation's progress. Look back at the annals of history, and you will find that the most significant reforms and achievements were the result of steadfast adherence to party principles.

In conclusion, I urge you to see party loyalty not as a shackle, but as a compass that guides elected officials in fulfilling their promises to the electorate, in achieving efficient governance, and in preserving the ideologies that are the cornerstone of our political system.

Therefore, ladies and gentlemen, I stand firmly against the motion. In a world where constancy and commitment are ever so rare, let us not undervalue the steadfastness that party loyalty brings to our democratic institutions. It is this loyalty that keeps the wheels of progress turning, ensuring that the voice of the people is not just heard, but acted upon.

Thank you.

Summary of the opposition's arguments

I. Effective Governance Through Party Unity
A. Party loyalty as a means to efficient policy implementation
- Examples where party unity expedited the legislative process.
- Case studies of countries with strong party loyalty leading to quicker policy decisions.
B. Prevention of political stalemate and gridlock
- Instances where party divisions led to legislative standstills.
- Analysis of governments with high levels of party loyalty experiencing fewer deadlocks.
II. Representation of the Electorate's Mandate
A. Political parties as a reflection of voters' choices
- Voters elect representatives based on party platforms and promises.
- Survey data showing public expectation for elected officials to follow party lines.
B. Accountability to the electoral base
- Case studies where politicians who strayed from party lines were seen as betraying their voters.
- Examples of elected officials losing support for not adhering to party principles.
III. Preservation of Political Ideologies and Long-term Goals

A. Maintaining ideological consistency
- How party loyalty ensures adherence to a consistent set of beliefs and policies.
- Historical examples of parties losing their core identity due to lack of loyalty.
B. Fulfillment of long-term strategic goals
- Examples of parties achieving long-term objectives through sustained loyalty.
- Analysis of successful long-term policies attributed to consistent party support.

10 questions from the coalition to the opposition:

1. How do you address the risk of party loyalty leading to the suppression of individual conscience and the erosion of democratic debate within the party?

2. What mechanisms are in place to prevent party loyalty from descending into blind allegiance, potentially leading to unethical or undemocratic actions?

3. How can party loyalty ensure the representation of diverse opinions within the electorate, considering that a single party's agenda might not reflect the views of all its supporters?

4. In instances where party policies conflict with constitutional principles, how should elected officials reconcile this conflict while maintaining party loyalty?

5. Can you provide examples where party loyalty has significantly improved the long-term welfare of the country, rather than just achieving short-term party goals?

6. How does prioritizing party loyalty over constitutional duty uphold the principles of checks and balances, a fundamental aspect of many democracies?

7. How do you propose to maintain public trust in situations where party loyalty leads to decisions that are unpopular or detrimental to certain segments of the populace?

8. In what ways does party loyalty contribute to constructive, bipartisan dialogue and cooperation, rather than fostering division and partisanship?

9. How can an elected official remain loyal to their party while ensuring that their actions do not infringe upon the rights and freedoms guaranteed by the constitution?

10. What measures can be taken to ensure that party loyalty does not lead to the stagnation of political progress, especially in cases where party agendas are misaligned with evolving societal needs?

10 questions from the opposition to the coalition:

1. How do you propose to manage situations where the constitution's interpretation is subjective and open to multiple readings, potentially leading to gridlock?

2. In what ways can prioritizing constitutional duty over party loyalty address the immediate and practical needs of governance, especially in crisis situations?

3. How would you ensure that elected officials don't use the guise of constitutional duty to justify actions that are actually driven by personal or ideological motives?

4. What is your response to the argument that party loyalty is essential for maintaining a clear and consistent policy direction, which can be lost in overly broad constitutional interpretations?

5. How do you reconcile situations where the constitutional principles seem out of step with current societal needs or values?

6. Can you provide historical examples where prioritizing constitutional duty over party loyalty has led to significant and tangible benefits for the nation?

7. How do you address concerns that excessive focus on constitutional duty could lead to neglect of the specific mandates and platforms on which politicians were elected?

8. In what ways does prioritizing constitutional duty facilitate effective bipartisan cooperation, rather than fostering ideological rigidity?

9. How do you propose to balance the need for constitutional adherence with the practicalities of political compromise, which is often necessary in governance?

10. How can an elected official ensure that their adherence to constitutional duty does not alienate them from their party, potentially undermining their ability to effectively advocate for their constituents' interests?

Potential solutions to reconcile the two parties

In the spirited debate between the coalition and the opposition, finding common ground may seem challenging, but with thoughtful consideration, we can identify potential solutions that respect both parties' concerns. The key to this lies in crafting compromises that balance constitutional duty with party loyalty, ensuring effective governance while upholding democratic principles.

One such solution is the **establishment of bipartisan committees**. These committees would be tasked with reviewing major policy decisions, ensuring they align with both constitutional values and party ideologies. This approach respects the opposition's emphasis on party agendas while ensuring the coalition's focus on constitutional adherence.

Furthermore, introducing **regular constitutional review processes** could help both sides. This process would involve both parties and aim to interpret constitutional principles in the context of contemporary challenges, ensuring the document remains a living, evolving guide that reflects societal changes. This respects the coalition's view of the constitution as a dynamic framework while allowing the opposition to ensure that party values are considered in its interpretation.

Another compromise lies in the **implementation of a mechanism for ethical oversight**. This would involve an independent body tasked with ensuring that all decisions by elected officials, whether influenced by party loyalty or constitutional duty, meet certain ethical standards. This solution addresses the coalition's concern for ethical governance while assuring the opposition that party loyalty is exercised within ethical boundaries.

To address concerns about policy consistency, there could be an emphasis on **developing long-term, bipartisan policy frameworks**. These frameworks would blend the party's immediate goals with broader constitutional principles, ensuring stability and continuity in governance.

The idea of **rotational leadership within key committees** could also be a viable compromise. This would ensure that both parties have the opportunity to lead and influence decision-making processes, respecting the opposition's emphasis on party representation while ensuring that constitutional principles are not sidelined.

In addition, **training programs for elected officials** on constitutional principles and the importance of party loyalty could bridge the understanding gap between both sides. Such programs would emphasize the importance of balancing these two elements in decision-making processes.

Moreover, the introduction of **'Constitutionality Impact Assessments' for new policies** could be a way forward. This would involve evaluating how well new policies align with constitutional principles, a nod to the coalition's priorities, while also considering the party's goals, respecting the opposition's stance.

To further ensure that party loyalty does not override constitutional duty, there could be a system of **public forums and consultations**. These would involve citizens in the decision-making process, ensuring that the government remains responsive to the electorate's needs while adhering to constitutional values.

Another solution might be the **establishment of a mediation panel** for instances where party loyalty and constitutional duty conflict. This panel, comprising members from both sides of the political spectrum, would work to find a middle ground in such cases.

Lastly, **regular performance reviews of elected officials**, based on their ability to balance party loyalty with constitutional duty, could be instituted. This would encourage politicians to strive for a balance between these two facets of their role, ensuring accountability to both their party and the constitution.

By weaving these solutions into the fabric of governance, we create a narrative of cooperation and mutual respect, addressing the key concerns of both the coalition and the opposition. This holistic approach paves the way for more effective and principled governance, where the duties to both party and constitution are harmoniously balanced.

Recommended Resources

Liberal Loyalty[4] by Anna Stilz

Coalition/Opposition Breakdown: 70/30

This book leans more towards the coalition's perspective, as it defends a liberal understanding of citizenship, emphasizing constitutional principles and civic obligations that go beyond just territorial, linguistic, or cultural aspects. Stilz argues that constitutional principles themselves justify obedience to a state, aligning with the coalition's view of prioritizing constitutional duty. However, there is also recognition of the role of democratic participation and national culture, which gives some credence to the opposition's emphasis on political loyalty.

Party Discipline in the U.S. House of Representatives[5] by Kathryn Pearson

Coalition/Opposition Breakdown: 30/70

This book leans towards the opposition's viewpoint. It discusses how party leaders command loyalty from members in various aspects

---

[4] https://amzn.to/3TpSNM3
[5] https://amzn.to/3ToAQ0v

like voting and contributions, and how this loyalty is rewarded or penalized, aligning with the opposition's argument for political loyalty. However, it also acknowledges the consequences of this discipline, such as legislative gridlock and the risk to democratic representation, which slightly aligns with the coalition's concerns about prioritizing party loyalty over constitutional duty.

Chapter 2: Media's Role in Shaping Political Narratives

Analyzing how media biases and misinformation influence public opinion and political outcomes.

The most polarizing aspect in the debate about the media's role in shaping political narratives lies in the issue of media bias and its influence on public opinion and political outcomes. This contentious point stems from the concern that media outlets, whether mainstream or alternative, may promote particular political agendas, influencing the public's perception and understanding of political events and issues.

The heart of the conflict revolves around the perception of media as either a manipulator or a messenger. On one side of the debate, there's a belief that media outlets are inherently biased, selectively presenting information to sway public opinion in favor of certain political ideologies or parties. This viewpoint argues that media bias leads to the spread of misinformation, shaping a political narrative that aligns with the interests of the media outlet's ownership or editorial stance, rather than presenting an objective view of the facts.

Opposing this, there are those who argue that the media's role is to inform the public, and that any perceived biases are either a reflection of the inherent diversity of perspectives in a free society or are exaggerated claims used by political entities to discredit reporting that is unfavorable to them. This view holds that media bias is not as pervasive or influential as claimed, suggesting that the public is capable of critical thinking and discerning fact from opinion.

The intensity of this debate is fueled by the significant impact that media narratives can have on public opinion and, consequently, on political elections and policies. Those who are concerned about media bias worry that a lack of objective reporting can undermine the democratic process, leading to a misinformed public and the potential manipulation of democratic outcomes. Conversely, defenders of the media argue that a diverse and free press is essential for democracy, allowing for a range of viewpoints and critical scrutiny of those in power.

This divisive issue is further complicated by the rise of social media and digital news platforms, which have transformed the way news is disseminated and consumed. The proliferation of these platforms has led to concerns about the echo chamber effect, where individuals only engage with information that conforms to their existing beliefs, potentially exacerbating divisions and polarization in society.

In summary, the central point of contention in the role of media in shaping political narratives is the balance between the media's influence as a potential source of bias and misinformation and its role as a critical informant of the public. This debate provokes strong reactions because it touches on fundamental questions about the nature of truth, freedom of expression, and the health of democratic societies.

Progressive and Conservative Viewpoints:

Identify the Progressive Viewpoint:

Aspect: The progressive viewpoint in this debate typically aligns with the argument that media bias is not as pervasive or influential as some claim, and that the media plays a crucial role in informing the public and holding power to account.

Justification: This aspect is considered progressive due to its emphasis on the importance of a diverse and free press as a tool for social reform and change. Progressives often stress the necessity of challenging established power structures and the role of media in promoting a variety of perspectives, especially those of marginalized groups. This viewpoint also aligns with progressive ideologies through its advocacy for critical thinking and individual discernment, suggesting that the public can navigate media narratives independently and benefit from exposure to a range of viewpoints.

Identify the Conservative Viewpoint:

Aspect: The conservative viewpoint often gravitates towards the belief that media outlets can be inherently biased, selectively presenting information to promote specific political ideologies or parties, thereby influencing public opinion and political outcomes in a way that might undermine traditional values or established norms.

Justification: This perspective is considered conservative as it frequently emphasizes the preservation of traditional values and the potential threats posed by perceived media bias to these values. Conservatives often argue for the importance of historical context and the risks associated with media narratives that might lead to rapid or uncontrolled social changes. Additionally, this viewpoint frequently underscores the need to maintain established norms and societal structures, expressing concern that media bias could lead to misinformation and a disruption of the traditional democratic process.

Political Analysis

Progressive/Liberal (Left) Viewpoints:

In Support of Media as a Critical Informant (Progressive Aspect): A significant portion of the left likely views the media as a crucial tool for democracy and social reform. They might believe in the media's role in challenging power structures and advocating for marginalized voices. This group likely forms the majority within the progressive camp, possibly around 70%. They emphasize critical thinking, individual discernment, and the need for a variety of perspectives in the media.

In Support of Concerns Over Media Bias (Conservative Aspect): There is a smaller segment within the left that might share concerns over media bias, particularly in how it could influence public opinion or propagate misinformation. This group, possibly making up about 30%, might stress the importance of maintaining factual reporting and caution against media narratives that could mislead the public or undermine democratic processes.

Conservative/Republican (Right) Viewpoints:

In Support of Media as a Critical Informant (Progressive Aspect): A minority within the conservative camp might recognize the importance of a diverse media landscape. They could acknowledge that while biases exist, the media plays an essential role in informing the public and ensuring a range of viewpoints is represented. This group might comprise about 20% of conservatives, emphasizing the need for a balanced approach to media consumption and critical analysis of information sources.

In Support of Concerns Over Media Bias (Conservative Aspect): The majority of conservatives, possibly around 80%, might align with the view that media bias is a significant issue. This group is likely to be concerned about the influence of media on public opinion, particularly in swaying it away from traditional values or conservative ideologies. They might advocate for a more balanced media representation and express skepticism about the current media landscape's ability to provide unbiased information.

---

[6] https://www.pewresearch.org/journalism/2023/04/18/podcasts-as-a-source-of-news-and-information/

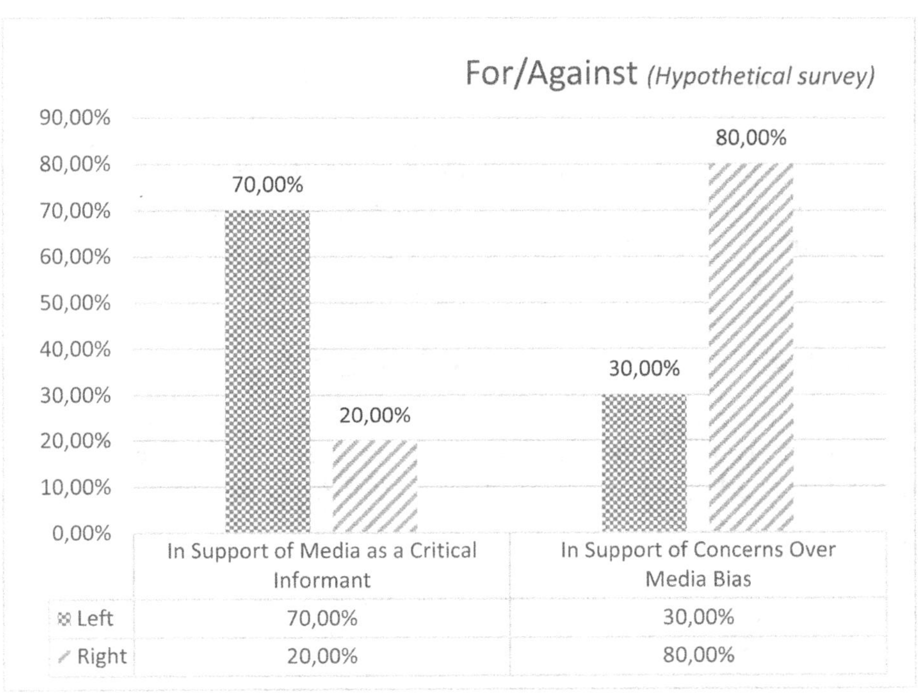

For/Against *(Hypothetical survey)*

	In Support of Media as a Critical Informant	In Support of Concerns Over Media Bias
Left	70,00%	30,00%
Right	20,00%	80,00%

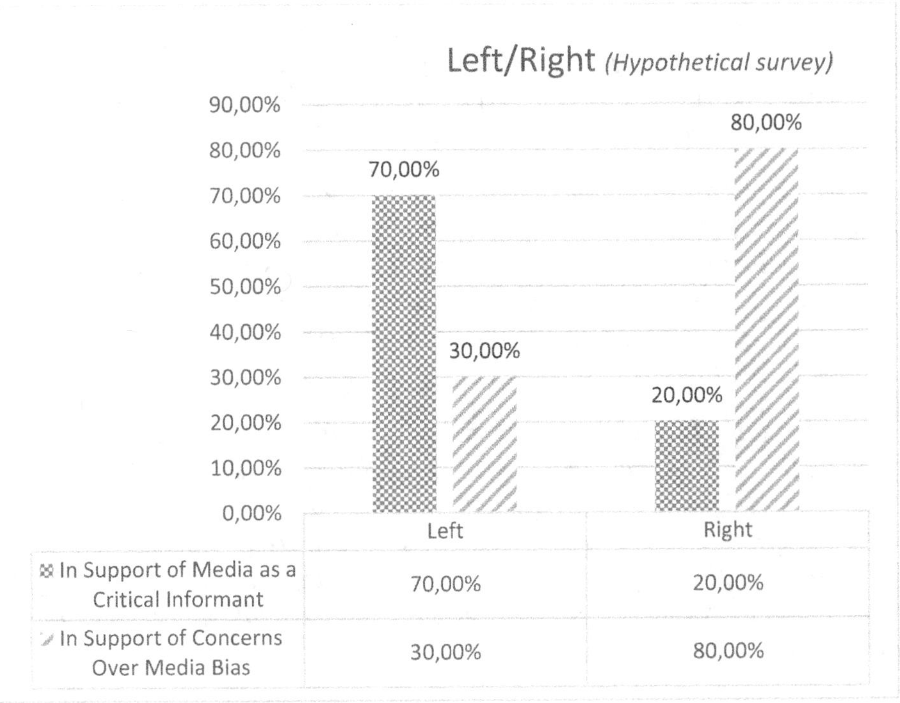

Left/Right *(Hypothetical survey)*

	Left	Right
In Support of Media as a Critical Informant	70,00%	20,00%
In Support of Concerns Over Media Bias	30,00%	80,00%

Motions of the debate

Coalition's Motion (Progressive Viewpoint):

"This house supports the view that a diverse and free press is essential for democracy, advocating for media's role in informing the public and promoting a variety of perspectives, especially those of marginalized groups."

Opposition's Motion (Conservative Viewpoint):

"This house opposes the prevailing media narratives that potentially undermine traditional values and societal norms, emphasizing the need for media to present unbiased information and maintain balanced reporting."

Coalition Speech

Ladies and gentlemen, esteemed judges, and fellow debaters, today we gather to discuss not just a matter of policy, but a cornerstone of our democracy. We stand to affirm that a diverse and free press is essential for a thriving democratic society.

Imagine a world where your voice, your struggles, and your triumphs find no echo in the media you consume. Where the manifold narratives of a diverse society are condensed into a monolithic perspective that serves the few. This is the world we reject. We believe in a media landscape as diverse as the society it serves, a platform where every voice, especially those marginalized, finds representation.

Let us consider the role of media as a facilitator of informed citizenship. Information is the lifeblood of democracy, and a diverse media ensures this lifeblood flows freely and fairly. Reflect upon moments in history where an informed public, armed with unvarnished truth from fearless journalism, stood up to challenge tyrants and spark social change. Remember Watergate, where investigative journalism played a pivotal role in upholding the sanctity of the American presidency.

But our argument does not merely dwell in the past. It lives and breathes in the ongoing struggles of our society. Media amplification of marginalized voices has been crucial in advancing causes from civil rights to environmental justice. When the media shines a light on inequality, it does more than report – it advocates for a better, more equitable world.

Yet, let us not forget the role of the media in fostering critical thinking. In an age where information is abundant, the ability to analyze and critique this information becomes paramount. A diverse media environment challenges us to think, question, and grow. It shields us from the echo chambers that threaten to fragment our society, offering instead a kaleidoscope of views that enrich our understanding and empathy.

In closing, I urge you to consider what kind of society we are fostering. Do we want a society that retreats into the comfort of uniformity, or one that embraces the messy, beautiful diversity of humanity? A vote for this motion is a vote for a society that values truth, encourages critical thinking, and believes in the power of diverse voices to shape a just and equitable world.

Thank you.

Summary of the coalition's arguments

I. The Necessity of a Diverse and Free Press for a Healthy Democracy
A. Facilitates Informed Citizenship
- Access to a variety of perspectives enables citizens to make more informed decisions.
- Studies show that societies with a free press exhibit higher levels of political participation.
B. Acts as a Check on Power
- Media scrutiny holds public officials and institutions accountable.
- Historical examples, like Watergate, demonstrate the media's role in uncovering government corruption.
II. Promotion of Marginalized Voices and Social Reform
A. Amplifies Underrepresented Perspectives
- Media diversity ensures representation of minority and marginalized groups.

- Case studies of social movements show how media coverage can elevate critical issues (e.g., Civil Rights Movement).
B. Catalyst for Progressive Change
- Media narratives can drive awareness and support for social reform.
- The role of media in advocating for LGBTQ+ rights and environmental issues serves as evidence.
III. Critical Thinking and Public Discernment
A. Encourages Analytical Skills
- Exposure to varied viewpoints fosters critical thinking and skepticism.
- Research indicates that diverse media exposure correlates with improved analytical thinking.
B. Mitigates Echo Chamber Effect
- A diverse media landscape counters the risks of information bubbles.
- Studies on social media and news consumption patterns illustrate the dangers of echo chambers and the benefits of diverse sources.

Opposition Speech

Ladies and gentlemen, esteemed judges, and audience, today we stand at a crucial crossroads in our debate about the essence of media and its impact on our society. Our opposition firmly believes that the unchecked rise of biased media narratives poses a significant threat to our cherished traditions and the very fabric of our democracy.

Firstly, let us address the undeniable impact of media bias on public opinion. Time and again, we have witnessed how selective reporting and skewed narratives have swayed public perception, often away from the truth. The power of the media to shape minds is immense, and with great power comes great responsibility – a responsibility that is being neglected. Consider the instances of misinformation during public health crises, where biased reporting led to confusion and harm, instead of clarity and safety.

Moving to the preservation of our traditional values and norms, it is crucial to understand the role of media in reflecting and upholding the societal values that bind us. A media that is bent on pushing a certain agenda, without regard for the existing norms and values, can lead to societal rifts and a breakdown of the social fabric. We advocate for a balanced approach where progress and tradition coexist, not where one is sacrificed for the other.

Lastly, the cornerstone of our argument rests on the need for balanced and unbiased reporting. The ideal role of media should be as a neutral informant, providing news and information without a tint of bias. This unbiased approach is not just idealistic but necessary for the functioning of a well-informed society. We have seen the positive impact of neutral reporting in fostering a well-rounded understanding of issues, leading to healthy public discourse.

In conclusion, while we recognize the importance of a free press, it is the unchecked bias and disregard for traditional values in current media practices that we stand against. We urge you to consider the long-term implications of a biased media landscape and join us in advocating for a return to balanced, responsible journalism. A vote against this motion is a vote for preserving the integrity of our information landscape and, ultimately, the health of our democratic society.

Thank you.

Summary of the opposition's arguments

I. Risk of Media Bias and Misinformation
A. Influence on Public Opinion
- Instances where media bias has swayed public opinion on political issues.
- Studies showing a correlation between media consumption and political perspectives.
B. Spread of Misinformation
- Examples of misinformation leading to public harm (e.g., during public health crises).
- Analysis of how misinformation can spread rapidly via biased reporting.
II. Preservation of Traditional Values and Norms
A. Media's Role in Cultural Continuity
- The importance of media in reflecting and preserving societal values and traditions.

- Case studies where media narratives have clashed with cultural norms, causing societal rifts.
B. Balance Between Progress and Tradition
- The need for media to maintain a balance between advocating for change and respecting existing values.
- Examples where rapid change driven by media narratives has led to social upheaval.
III. Ensuring Balanced and Unbiased Reporting
A. Media as a Neutral Informant
- The ideal role of media as an unbiased provider of news and information.
- Instances where neutral reporting has positively impacted public understanding and discourse.
B. Challenges in Achieving Media Neutrality
- The difficulty in eliminating biases due to ownership, funding sources, or political affiliations.
- Analysis of media systems in different countries showing varying levels of bias and their impact on society.

10 questions from the coalition to the opposition:

1. How do you reconcile the need for unbiased reporting with the inherent subjectivity of human perspective in journalism?

2. What mechanisms would you propose to ensure media neutrality without infringing on the freedom of the press?

3. How can we differentiate between preserving traditional values and suppressing progressive voices in media narratives?

4. In what ways do you think a media that focuses heavily on traditional values might inadvertently contribute to societal stagnation or regression?

5. Can you provide examples of unbiased media sources, and explain how they successfully achieve this neutrality?

6. How would you address the concern that emphasizing traditional values in media could marginalize underrepresented groups and their perspectives?

7. What criteria would you use to determine if media content is balanced, and who should be responsible for this determination?

8. How do you propose to handle the challenge of media echo chambers in a landscape that emphasizes traditional values, which might not always be inclusive?

9. Can you elaborate on how a media focused on traditional values would report on issues that challenge these values, such as LGBTQ+ rights or climate change?

10. How would you ensure that the pursuit of unbiased reporting does not lead to false equivalence, where fringe or unfounded viewpoints are given equal weight as well-researched, factual information?

10 questions from the opposition to the coalition:

1. How do you propose to manage the risk of media echo chambers, which can be exacerbated by a press that primarily amplifies marginalized voices?

2. What criteria would you suggest for determining when media representation of marginalized groups crosses from advocacy into bias?

3. How would you address the concern that emphasizing diverse perspectives might lead to the dilution or misrepresentation of factual information?

4. Can you provide concrete examples where a diverse media has successfully led to significant social reform without compromising journalistic integrity?

5. In promoting diverse viewpoints, how would you ensure that extremist or harmful ideologies are not given a platform under the guise of media diversity?

6. How do you propose to balance the need for media diversity with the necessity of a cohesive societal narrative that unites rather than divides?

7. What measures would you recommend to prevent the media from becoming an echo chamber for progressive ideologies at the expense of other perspectives?

8. How can media ensure the representation of diverse viewpoints without falling into the trap of presenting false equivalency between well-founded and fringe perspectives?

9. Can you explain how a diverse and free press would handle reporting on issues where the majority public opinion is in opposition to progressive ideals?

10. How would you address the potential for media bias in favor of progressive viewpoints, given the human tendency towards subjective interpretation?

Potential solutions to reconcile the two parties

In the quest to harmonize the diverse views of the coalition and the opposition, we embark on a journey to find common ground, a space where the ideals of a free, diverse press can coexist with the preservation of traditional values and balanced reporting.

We begin by recognizing the **importance of editorial independence.** Both sides can agree that media should operate free from undue influence, whether from government or private interests. This independence is crucial in ensuring that media can serve its role effectively, be it as a watchdog or a reflector of societal values.

A solution that respects both viewpoints is the establishment of a **media ombudsman** or an independent review board. This body could oversee complaints and concerns about media bias, ensuring accountability and transparency. By having diverse representation within this body, both the coalition and the opposition can have their concerns addressed fairly.

Another common ground lies in the **education of media consumers.** Both sides can support initiatives to educate the public on media literacy. This approach empowers individuals to critically analyze and interpret media content, fostering discernment that transcends biases.

The coalition and opposition might also find agreement in the **promotion of diverse media ownership**. This could involve encouraging the growth of independent media outlets and supporting community-based media, ensuring a wide range of perspectives and mitigating the risk of any single narrative dominating the media landscape.

Further, there is room for consensus on the **ethical standards of journalism**. Both sides can endorse rigorous journalistic standards that emphasize fact-checking, fairness, and the distinction between news and opinion. Such standards can serve as a bulwark against misinformation, irrespective of the source.

The coalition and opposition could also explore the potential of a **shared media platform**. This platform could be a space where journalists from different backgrounds and ideologies contribute, providing a balanced mix of perspectives. It would be a symbolic and practical embodiment of media diversity and neutrality.

In recognizing the power of algorithms in shaping media consumption, both sides can advocate for **transparent algorithmic processes** in digital media platforms. This transparency can help users understand how and why certain content is recommended to them, enabling better control over their media diet.

Acknowledging the concern over marginalized voices, a **community outreach program** led by media organizations could be a point of agreement. This program would involve actively seeking out stories and perspectives from a variety of communities, ensuring that their voices are heard and represented.

To address concerns over rapid social change, a **dialogue series** featuring voices from across the spectrum can be initiated. This would be a platform for discussing how media narratives intersect with societal values, promoting understanding and empathy among different groups.

Lastly, both sides can agree on the value of **periodic media impact assessments**. Conducted by independent bodies, these assessments can evaluate how media is affecting society, providing insights that guide future media practices and policies.

In weaving these solutions into the fabric of our media landscape, we create a tapestry rich with diversity, yet grounded in a shared commitment to truth, accountability, and respect for varying perspectives. This is the path towards a media that not only informs and reflects society but also unites and strengthens it.

Recommended Resources

The Hype Machine: How Social Media Disrupts Our Elections, Our Economy, and Our Health—and How We Must Adapt by Sinan Aral

Coalition/Opposition Breakdown: 60/40

Aral's work leans slightly towards the coalition's perspective by emphasizing the transformative impact of social media on various societal aspects. However, it also addresses concerns relevant to the opposition by discussing the negative effects of social media, including misinformation and its influence on elections.

The Presentation of Self in Everyday Life by Erving Goffman

Coalition/Opposition Breakdown: 70/30

While not directly about media, Goffman's exploration of identity creation aligns more with the coalition's emphasis on diverse perspectives and the role of media in shaping public perception. It delves into how individuals present themselves, relevant to understanding social media's influence on public opinion.

Uncivil Agreement: How Politics Became Our Identity by Lilliana Mason

Coalition/Opposition Breakdown: 50/50

Mason's book explores the depth of political polarization in the United States, offering insights into how deeply ingrained political identities have become, a point of interest for both sides of the debate.

Bit by Bit: Social Research in the Digital Age by Matthew Salganik

Coalition/Opposition Breakdown: 50/50

Salganik's book, focusing on social research methods in the digital era, provides a neutral, methodological perspective that is applicable to both the coalition's and opposition's concerns about the role and influence of media in society.

Chapter 3: The Historical Precedents of Election Disputes

Comparing the 2020 U.S. election dispute to past controversies, like the 1876 Tilden-Hayes election.

The historical precedents of election disputes, particularly when comparing the 2020 U.S. election dispute to past controversies like the 1876 Tilden-Hayes election, reveal a core aspect that stands at the heart of the debate: the legitimacy of election outcomes. This aspect is the most contentious and divisive, representing the primary point of disagreement or conflict.

The legitimacy of an election outcome becomes the focal point of contention due to its fundamental importance in a democratic system. It's not just about who wins or loses, but about the trust in the electoral process itself. The disputes arise when this trust is questioned, either through allegations of fraud, voter suppression, or the mishandling of votes.

In the case of the 2020 U.S. election, the dispute was primarily fueled by claims of widespread voter fraud and irregularities, which were vehemently debated across political spectrums. These claims led to numerous legal challenges and a significant portion of the population doubting the election's integrity. This echoed the 1876 Tilden-Hayes election, where the results were contested due to accusations of electoral fraud and the compromise that ultimately decided the presidency.

The reason why the legitimacy of election outcomes provokes such strong debate is deeply rooted in the democratic ideals of fairness, transparency, and the rule of law. On one hand, there are arguments emphasizing the need to investigate and address any allegations of fraud to maintain public trust in the electoral system. On the other hand, there are concerns that unfounded or disproved claims can undermine the democratic process and destabilize the political environment.

This dichotomy creates a highly charged atmosphere where the underlying issue transcends the specific details of the dispute and touches upon the very principles that uphold democratic governance. The debate becomes a reflection of the broader political and social divides, making the question of election legitimacy a lightning rod for deeper, more fundamental disagreements about the state of democracy and the rule of law.

Thus, the most polarizing aspect of historical election disputes, illustrated by the 2020 U.S. election and the 1876 Tilden-Hayes election, is the contention over the legitimacy of election outcomes. This aspect remains a potent source of division, highlighting the ongoing struggle to balance the integrity of the electoral process with the need to foster trust and unity in the democratic system.

Progressive and Conservative Viewpoints:

Identify the Progressive Viewpoint:

Aspect: The progressive viewpoint in this context often emphasizes the need for reforms in the electoral process to enhance fairness and inclusivity. This includes advocating for measures to prevent voter suppression, enhance the accessibility of voting, and ensure transparent and verifiable vote counting procedures.

Justification: This aspect is considered progressive due to its focus on change and modernization of the electoral system. It aligns with progressive ideologies that prioritize social reform, equality, and the adaptation of institutions to reflect contemporary societal values. Progressives often argue that the electoral system must evolve to address current challenges and to represent diverse populations fairly, seeing change and reform as necessary for the health and legitimacy of the democratic process.

Identify the Conservative Viewpoint:

Aspect: The conservative viewpoint typically centers on the importance of upholding established electoral laws and traditions, often expressing concern over rapid changes or reforms that might compromise the integrity of the election process. This includes a strong emphasis on preventing voter fraud and maintaining the traditional mechanisms and regulations of voting.

Justification: This perspective is considered conservative as it reflects a preference for preserving tradition and established norms. Conservative ideologies often emphasize the value of historical context and the maintenance of tried-and-tested systems. They tend to prioritize the rule of law and the existing structure of electoral processes, arguing that these have been effective in maintaining order and integrity in past elections. Conservatives often view rapid or extensive reforms with caution, concerned that such changes might lead to unintended consequences or undermine the stability and reliability of the electoral system.

To Know

Changes in U.S. Voting Rights: Following the Supreme Court's 2013 ruling that weakened Section 5 of the Voting Rights Act of 1965, there has been a surge in states enacting restrictive voting laws. Over 361 voter suppression bills have been introduced in 33 states, and 19 states have enacted 33 laws with such restrictions. These developments highlight the ongoing battle over voting rights and access in the U.S.[7]

---

[7] https://www.sir.advancedleadership.harvard.edu/articles/voting-rights-reforms-and-the-democracy-crisis

Progressive/Liberal (Left) Viewpoints:

In Support of Electoral Reforms and Inclusivity (Progressive Aspect of the Topic): A significant segment of the left likely views electoral reforms and inclusivity positively, advocating for changes to enhance fairness and accessibility in voting. This group might include those who are concerned about voter suppression and the representation of marginalized communities. Estimated percentage: 70%.

In Support of Upholding Established Electoral Laws (Conservative Aspect of the Topic): A smaller portion of the left might support maintaining established electoral laws and traditions, perhaps driven by a belief in the stability and integrity of the current system, or concerns about the feasibility and implications of rapid reforms. Estimated percentage: 30%.

Conservative/Republican (Right) Viewpoints:

In Support of Electoral Reforms and Inclusivity (Progressive Aspect of the Topic): Within the conservative camp, there could be a minority who are in favor of certain electoral reforms, possibly those who recognize the need for updating the system to address current challenges while still maintaining the overall structure. Estimated percentage: 20%.

In Support of Upholding Established Electoral Laws (Conservative Aspect of the Topic): The majority of conservatives likely favor preserving established electoral laws and traditions, emphasizing the prevention of voter fraud and the importance of maintaining traditional voting mechanisms and regulations. Estimated percentage: 80%.

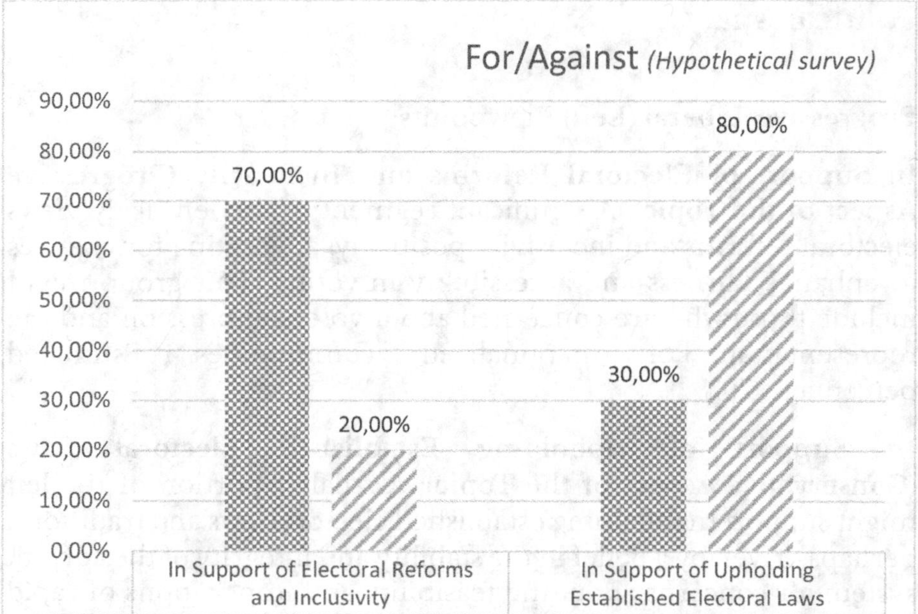

For/Against *(Hypothetical survey)*

	In Support of Electoral Reforms and Inclusivity	In Support of Upholding Established Electoral Laws
Left	70,00%	30,00%
Right	20,00%	80,00%

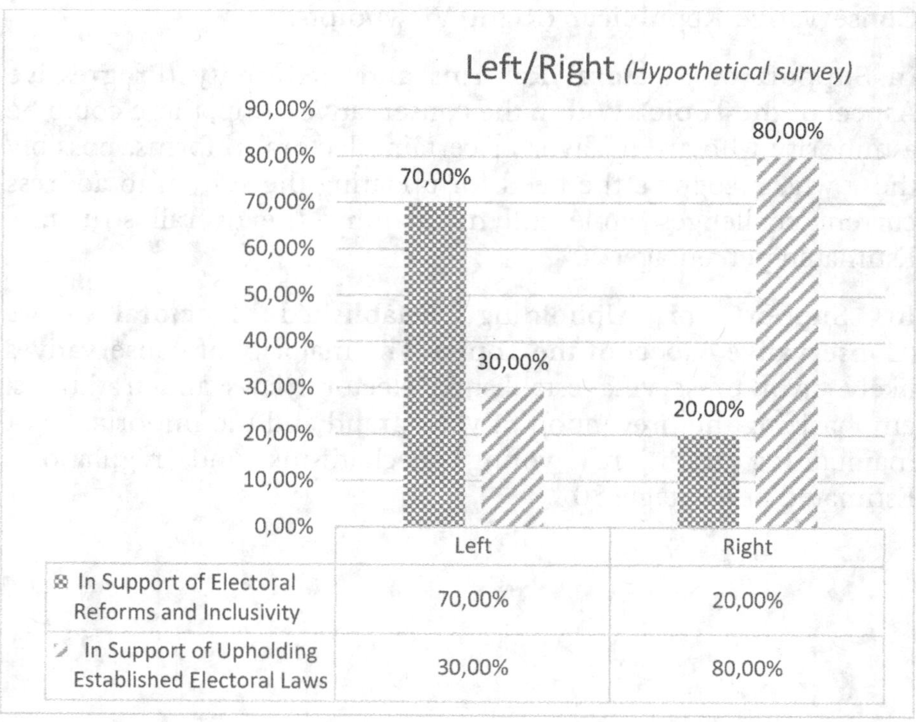

Left/Right *(Hypothetical survey)*

	Left	Right
In Support of Electoral Reforms and Inclusivity	70,00%	20,00%
In Support of Upholding Established Electoral Laws	30,00%	80,00%

Coalition's Motion (Progressive Viewpoint):

"This house supports comprehensive reforms to the electoral system to enhance fairness, inclusivity, and the integrity of democratic processes."

Opposition's Motion (Conservative Viewpoint):

"This house opposes any major reforms to the current electoral system, affirming the preservation of established electoral laws and traditions to maintain order and integrity."

Coalition Speech

Ladies and gentlemen, esteemed judges, and fellow debaters,

Today, I stand before you not just as a speaker, but as a champion of a cause that resonates at the core of our democracy – the need for comprehensive reforms in our electoral system. Our motion, "This house supports comprehensive reforms to enhance fairness, inclusivity, and integrity in democratic processes," is not just a statement. It's a call to action, a plea for progress, and a blueprint for a more inclusive and fair democracy.

Imagine a world where every voice is heard, where the marginalized are no longer sidelined, but given a platform to influence the very fabric of our society. This is not a utopian dream, but a tangible reality that can be achieved through electoral reforms. Our first argument hinges on enhancing democratic representation and fairness. Why? Because the essence of democracy is the voice of its people. We have witnessed, time and again, the pernicious effects of voter suppression, particularly in marginalized communities. Remember the Voting Rights Act of 1965? It wasn't just legislation; it was a beacon of hope, drastically increasing voter turnout in historically suppressed groups. And yet, today, we still see instances where stricter ID laws and polling place closures disproportionately affect minority voters. Our fight is to remove these barriers, to make voting not just a right but a reality for all.

But what about accessibility? We live in a world that is constantly evolving, and our electoral process must evolve with it. Consider the success stories from states with high mail-in voting, showing remarkable increases in participation. Look at countries with more accessible voting systems and their higher voter turnout rates. This isn't innovation for the sake of innovation; it's adapting to meet the needs of our time.

Moving to our second argument, we must discuss the integrity and trust in our electoral system. In an age rife with misinformation and cyber threats, can we afford to cling to outdated systems? When we talk about adapting to modern challenges, we're not just theorizing. There are examples where outdated systems were exploited for electoral fraud. But on the flip side, look at nations that have modernized their electoral processes effectively. These aren't just success stories; they're roadmaps for us to follow.

Building public trust is not an option; it's a necessity. Surveys consistently show public concern over election integrity. We've seen how increased transparency and oversight have led to higher public trust in election results. This isn't just about maintaining the status quo; it's about strengthening the very foundation of our democratic system.

Our final argument is a call to reflect contemporary societal values. Our society is not static; it's dynamic, diverse, and ever-changing. Our electoral system must mirror this diversity. We've seen historical examples where reforms led to more inclusive democracies. But it's not just about looking back; it's about looking forward. There's a societal shift towards a need for more representative electoral processes. And let's not forget the impact on political engagement. Data shows a clear correlation between inclusive voting laws and civic engagement. When people feel represented, they participate. When they participate, democracy thrives.

In conclusion, our motion is not just a debate topic. It's a vision for a future where every vote counts, where democracy is not just a concept but a lived experience for every citizen. We're not just advocating for change; we're advocating for progress, for a system that reflects who we are as a society today, and for a future that we can all be proud of.

Thank you.

Summary of the coalition's arguments

I. Enhancing Democratic Representation and Fairness
- A. Reducing Voter Suppression: Reforms are necessary to address and reduce instances of voter suppression, especially in marginalized communities.- The Voting Rights Act of 1965 and its impact on increasing voter turnout in historically suppressed groups.
- Recent instances where stricter ID laws and polling place closures disproportionately affected minority voters.
- The Voting Rights Act of 1965 and its impact on increasing voter turnout in historically suppressed groups.
- Recent instances where stricter ID laws and polling place closures disproportionately affected minority voters.
- B. Increasing Accessibility: Modernizing the voting process to make it more accessible, including mail-in voting and extended voting periods.- Success stories from states with high mail-in voting showing increased participation.
- Comparison of voter turnout rates in countries with more accessible voting systems.
- Success stories from states with high mail-in voting showing increased participation.
- Comparison of voter turnout rates in countries with more accessible voting systems.
II. Ensuring Integrity and Trust in the Electoral System
- A. Adapting to Modern Challenges: Updating electoral systems to address current challenges such as misinformation and cyber threats.- Examples of how outdated systems have been exploited for electoral fraud.
- Success stories of nations that have effectively modernized their electoral processes.
- Examples of how outdated systems have been exploited for electoral fraud.
- Success stories of nations that have effectively modernized their electoral processes.
- B. Building Public Trust: Implementing transparent processes and independent oversight to build and maintain public trust in elections.- Surveys showing public concern over election integrity.

- Case studies where increased transparency and oversight led to higher public trust in election results.
- Surveys showing public concern over election integrity.
- Case studies where increased transparency and oversight led to higher public trust in election results.
III. Promoting Progressive and Inclusive Democratic Norms
- A. Reflecting Contemporary Societal Values: Aligning the electoral system with contemporary values of inclusivity and equal representation.- Historical examples where electoral reforms led to more inclusive democracies.
- Societal shifts indicating a need for more representative electoral processes.
- Historical examples where electoral reforms led to more inclusive democracies.
- Societal shifts indicating a need for more representative electoral processes.
- B. Encouraging Political Engagement and Participation: Demonstrating that an inclusive and fair electoral system encourages broader political participation.- Data showing a correlation between inclusive voting laws and civic engagement.
- Examples of increased political activism following electoral reforms.
- Data showing a correlation between inclusive voting laws and civic engagement.
- Examples of increased political activism following electoral reforms.

Opposition Speech

Ladies and gentlemen, honorable judges, and esteemed audience,

Today, I stand before you not to oppose change for the sake of opposition, but to advocate for the wisdom of prudence, the value of stability, and the importance of proven systems in our democratic process. We, the opposition, firmly believe that maintaining our established electoral laws and traditions is paramount to preserving the integrity and order of our democratic system.

Let us begin with a fundamental truth: change, especially when hastily implemented, carries risks. When we speak of rapid reforms in our electoral system, we speak of a path paved with uncertainties and potential for errors and fraud. History is replete with examples where new voting technologies, rushed into practice, led to significant issues. These are not mere hypothetical scenarios; they are cautionary tales that remind us of the value of our time-tested systems.

Our current electoral framework is not a relic of the past; it is the bedrock upon which our democracy stands. Think of the numerous elections held over the years, their outcomes respected and accepted. This stability is not coincidental; it is the result of our adherence to established laws and procedures. When we delve into case studies across the globe, we find a common thread: nations that hold firm to their electoral traditions enjoy a continuity that underpins their democratic health.

Moreover, let us consider the rule of law. The fabric of our society is woven with the threads of legal frameworks developed and refined over generations. To disregard this heritage in favor of untested reforms is to risk unraveling the very tapestry of our democracy. Past electoral disputes, resolved within the confines of our existing laws, stand as testaments to their effectiveness and resilience.

But what of the practicality of implementing widespread electoral changes? The logistical challenges are immense, often underestimated. Studies and reports have shown the high costs, both financial and in terms of human resources, associated with overhauling electoral systems. This is not mere conjecture; these are realities that communities across our nation would have to face.

And let us not forget the voter, the cornerstone of our democracy. Consistency in our electoral process is not a sign of stagnation but a beacon of reliability for the voter. Time and again, surveys have shown that sudden changes in voting procedures can lead to confusion, disenfranchisement, and a decline in voter turnout. Our duty is to minimize disruption, to ensure that every citizen can exercise their right to vote without facing the hurdles of navigating an ever-shifting landscape.

In conclusion, our stance is not one of intransigence, but of thoughtful consideration for the pillars that uphold our democracy. We oppose the motion not because we fear change, but because we respect the legacy, the efficacy, and the sanctity of our current electoral system. We stand for a democracy that is stable, reliable, and proven, one that is the envy of the world not for its propensity for change, but for its unwavering commitment to the principles of order and integrity.

Thank you.

Summary of the opposition's arguments

I. Preserving Electoral Integrity and Stability
- A. Risk of Fraud in Rapid Reforms: Rapidly implementing new voting methods increases the risk of fraud and errors.- Examples of issues encountered in places that quickly adopted new voting technologies or processes.
- Studies showing a correlation between rapid electoral changes and increased vulnerabilities.
- Examples of issues encountered in places that quickly adopted new voting technologies or processes.
- Studies showing a correlation between rapid electoral changes and increased vulnerabilities.
- B. Maintaining Proven Systems: Historical stability and success of the current electoral systems.- Historical instances where established systems have ensured fair and reliable elections.
- Comparative analysis showing the effectiveness of traditional voting methods over newer, untested ones.
- Historical instances where established systems have ensured fair and reliable elections.
- Comparative analysis showing the effectiveness of traditional voting methods over newer, untested ones.
II. Upholding Democratic Traditions and Rule of Law
- A. Respecting Established Legal Frameworks: The importance of adhering to existing legal frameworks which have been developed over time.- Examples of past electoral disputes that were successfully resolved within the framework of existing laws.
- Case studies where changing electoral laws led to legal ambiguities and conflicts.
- Examples of past electoral disputes that were successfully resolved within the framework of existing laws.
- Case studies where changing electoral laws led to legal ambiguities and conflicts.

- B. Protecting Voter Sovereignty: Ensuring that changes to the electoral system are driven by voter mandate and not by political agendas.- Instances where electoral reforms were pushed without broad public support, leading to backlash.
- Surveys showing public satisfaction with current voting processes.
- Instances where electoral reforms were pushed without broad public support, leading to backlash.
- Surveys showing public satisfaction with current voting processes.
III. Ensuring Practical and Feasible Implementation
- A. Logistical Challenges of Rapid Reforms: The practical difficulties in implementing widespread electoral changes, including costs and training.- Case studies of logistical failures when introducing new voting systems.
- Budget analyses demonstrating the high costs of overhauling electoral systems.
- Case studies of logistical failures when introducing new voting systems.
- Budget analyses demonstrating the high costs of overhauling electoral systems.
- B. Minimizing Disruption to Voters: Reducing confusion and inconvenience to voters by maintaining consistent voting processes.- Surveys showing voter confusion or difficulties adapting to new voting methods.
- Examples where changes in voting procedures led to lower voter turnout due to uncertainty or lack of information.
- Surveys showing voter confusion or difficulties adapting to new voting methods.
- Examples where changes in voting procedures led to lower voter turnout due to uncertainty or lack of information.

10 questions from the coalition to the opposition:

1. How do you address the concern that maintaining current electoral laws may perpetuate existing inequalities and fail to represent the evolving demographics of our society?

2. In what ways can a system that prioritizes tradition adapt to the challenges posed by modern technology, especially in preventing cyber threats and misinformation?

3. What evidence can you provide to show that the current electoral system adequately addresses the issue of voter suppression, particularly in marginalized communities?

4. How would you propose to deal with the logistical and practical challenges of ensuring voter integrity in an increasingly digital and interconnected world without reforming the electoral system?

5. Can you give examples of countries that have successfully maintained their traditional electoral systems without any reforms, while still managing to increase voter turnout and satisfaction?

6. How do you reconcile the need for stability in the electoral system with the growing public demand for more accessible and inclusive voting processes?

7. What measures would you suggest to ensure that the current electoral system remains relevant and effective in the face of rapidly changing societal norms and values?

8. In your view, how does the current electoral system effectively combat the risks of voter fraud, and are these measures sufficient in today's context?

9. How do you propose to enhance public trust in the electoral process while advocating for the preservation of the status quo, especially among those who feel disenfranchised by the current system?

10. Considering the advancements in technology and communication, how does the opposition plan to update the current electoral system to cope with these changes without implementing comprehensive reforms?

10 questions from the opposition to the coalition:

1. How do you plan to ensure that the proposed electoral reforms will not introduce new complexities and barriers that could inadvertently disenfranchise voters?

2. In what ways can the coalition guarantee that the modernization of the electoral system won't compromise the security and integrity of votes, considering the increasing threats of cyber-attacks and digital fraud?

3. What concrete evidence can you provide that suggests electoral reforms would lead to a significant increase in voter turnout and engagement, especially among marginalized communities?

4. How would you address the potential financial and logistical challenges that come with implementing widespread electoral reforms, particularly in underfunded and rural areas?

5. Can you cite examples of countries where similar electoral reforms have been implemented successfully without leading to increased polarization or political instability?

6. How does the coalition propose to balance the need for modernizing the electoral system with the risk of alienating older or less technologically savvy voters?

7. What measures would be in place to prevent the abuse of more accessible voting methods, such as mail-in voting or extended voting periods, from being exploited for electoral fraud?

8. How do you plan to ensure that the reforms you propose will be accepted and respected across the political spectrum, thereby maintaining the unity and stability of the nation?

9. In what ways can the coalition assure that the proposed reforms will not lead to an over-centralization of electoral processes, potentially diminishing local control and adaptability?

10. How will the coalition address concerns that rapid and comprehensive electoral reforms might lead to legal ambiguities and conflicts that could undermine public confidence in the electoral process?

Potential solutions to reconcile the two parties

In the pursuit of a common ground that respects the perspectives of both the coalition and the opposition, we find ourselves navigating a landscape ripe with opportunities for compromise and mutual understanding. At the heart of this journey lies the shared goal of a robust and fair electoral system, a goal that unites us despite our differing viewpoints.

Firstly, a key to resolving our differences lies in the **gradual implementation of reforms**. Instead of sweeping changes, we can introduce small, measured modifications to the electoral process. This approach respects the opposition's concerns about preserving stability while addressing the coalition's desire for progress and modernization.

Within this framework, we might consider the **introduction of pilot programs** in select regions. These pilots could test the viability of new voting technologies or methods, such as mail-in voting, before a wider rollout. By doing so, we ensure a careful evaluation of their impact, balancing the need for innovation with the wisdom of caution.

Another area ripe for compromise is the **enhancement of voter education programs**. These initiatives could focus on both traditional and new voting methods, ensuring all demographics are comfortable and familiar with the processes. This approach addresses the coalition's focus on inclusivity and the opposition's concern for maintaining voter confidence in the system.

Further, it is crucial to establish **bipartisan oversight committees** to oversee these reforms. These committees would ensure that changes are made transparently and with input from all political spectrums, thereby maintaining the integrity and trust that are fundamental to both parties.

In terms of security, a middle ground could be found in the **collaboration with technology experts** to safeguard the electoral process. By leveraging new technologies for security rather than just voting methods, we can modernize our system in a way that addresses the coalition's call for adaptation while alleviating the opposition's concerns about the risks of rapid reform.

The **incremental introduction of online or digital voting options** for certain categories of voters, such as overseas citizens or military personnel, could also be a step forward. This would be a cautious foray into modern voting methods, allowing time to assess and refine these systems.

On the financial front, a solution lies in **phased funding strategies** for electoral reform. Instead of a significant one-time investment, a gradual increase in funding allows for more manageable budgeting and demonstrates fiscal responsibility.

Moreover, we should also focus on **strengthening current laws against voter suppression and fraud**, satisfying both the coalition's desire for fairness and the opposition's emphasis on law and order. This could involve revising existing regulations or enhancing enforcement mechanisms.

In addressing concerns over voter participation, both sides might agree on the importance of **national campaigns to encourage voter turnout**. These campaigns, focusing on the importance of civic engagement, would address the coalition's goal of increased participation without altering the fundamental structure of the electoral process.

Lastly, the establishment of a **joint task force to regularly review and suggest improvements** to the electoral system could provide ongoing oversight and adaptation. This body would ensure that the electoral system remains responsive to the needs of society, technology, and the law.

In weaving these solutions into our shared narrative, we craft not just a series of compromises, but a tapestry of democratic resilience. This approach allows us to honor tradition while embracing progress, ensuring that our electoral system reflects the best of both viewpoints.

Recommended Resources

The Politics of Electoral Reform: Changing the Rules of Democracy[8] by Renwick, Alan

Coalition/Opposition Breakdown: 60/40

This book leans slightly towards the coalition's perspective, highlighting how voters and reform activists can impact electoral reform, which aligns with the coalition's advocacy for change and modernization in the electoral system.

Defining Democracy: Electoral Reform and the Struggle for Power in New York City[9] by Daniel O. Prosterman

Coalition/Opposition Breakdown: 50/50

This book treats the subject neutrally, examining the struggles over electoral reform in the context of democracy's evolution in the United States and globally. This balanced approach offers insights into both the need for reforms and the challenges associated with them, making it equally relevant to both sides of the debate.

Why Do We Still Have the Electoral College?[10] by Alexander Keyssar

Coalition/Opposition Breakdown: 40/60

This book leans slightly towards the opposition's viewpoint, as it delves into the history and rationale behind maintaining a unique aspect of the U.S. electoral system, the Electoral College. Its focus on this traditional element of the electoral system aligns more with the opposition's emphasis on preserving established systems.

---

[8] https://amzn.to/47WSmgz
[9] https://amzn.to/41tDFPS
[10] https://amzn.to/3TpolBD

Race, Reform, and Regulation of the Electoral Process: Recurring Puzzles in American Democracy[11] edited by Guy-Uriel E. Charles, Heather K. Gerken & Michael S. Kang

Coalition/Opposition Breakdown: 70/30

This book is more aligned with the coalition's position. It critically evaluates themes like the relationship between race and politics, and the performance and reform of election systems, issues that are typically emphasized by those advocating for electoral reforms and greater inclusivity in the voting process.

Electoral Systems and Democracy[12] edited by Larry Diamond & Marc F. Plattner

Coalition/Opposition Breakdown: 50/50

This book provides a balanced examination of electoral systems and democracy, addressing the debate among experts about which systems best promote the consolidation of democracy. This balanced exploration is relevant to both sides, offering perspectives on both maintaining stability and considering reforms.

---

[11] https://amzn.to/3Ntakzf
[12] https://amzn.to/3Tq723A

Chapter 4: The Balance of Power Between Executive and Legislative Branches

Examining the separation of powers in the context of presidential overreach.

The most polarizing aspect of the balance of power between the executive and legislative branches, particularly in the context of presidential overreach, revolves around the interpretation and limits of executive power. This contention lies at the heart of many debates, as it directly impacts the functioning of democratic governance and the preservation of checks and balances.

The central issue is the extent to which a president can exercise authority without overstepping the boundaries set by the Constitution and Congress. This is a highly divisive topic because it touches upon the fundamental principles of separation of powers and the rule of law. On one side of the debate, there are those who argue for a strong executive branch, emphasizing the need for decisive and efficient leadership, especially in times of crisis. This viewpoint holds that a certain degree of latitude should be given to the president, allowing for swift and unilateral decisions when necessary. Proponents of this perspective often cite historical instances where presidential assertiveness was crucial in addressing national challenges.

On the other side, there are those who advocate for strict limits on presidential power, emphasizing the dangers of authoritarianism and the importance of legislative oversight. This camp argues that unchecked executive power undermines the democratic process and risks leading to abuses of power. They often point to examples where presidential actions, taken without sufficient consultation or approval from Congress, have led to controversial or unconstitutional outcomes.

The heart of this contention lies in how the Constitution's provisions are interpreted. While some view the document as granting expansive powers to the president, others see it as setting clear boundaries to prevent any overreach. This debate is not just theoretical but has practical implications, influencing policy decisions, legal battles, and the overall trust in governmental institutions.

This issue provokes strong debate because it directly affects the balance of power within the government and has a lasting impact on the democratic system. The controversy is further fueled by differing political ideologies, historical precedents, and contemporary challenges that test the limits of executive power. As such, the debate over presidential overreach and the balance of power between the executive and legislative branches remains a contentious and central aspect of political discourse, reflecting deeper questions about the nature and limits of governmental authority in a democracy.

Progressive and Conservative Viewpoints:

Identify the Progressive Viewpoint:

Aspect: Advocacy for strict limits on presidential power and emphasizing legislative oversight.

Justification: This aspect is considered progressive because it often aligns with ideologies that prioritize checks and balances in government, aiming to prevent authoritarianism and promote democratic accountability. Progressives typically emphasize the need for constant vigilance against the concentration of power, advocating for a modern interpretation of the Constitution that adapts to contemporary challenges. This perspective often involves a focus on social reform and ensuring that government actions do not infringe upon civil liberties and equality. It reflects a belief in evolving governance structures to address current societal needs and potential governmental overreach.

Identify the Conservative Viewpoint:

Aspect: Support for a strong executive branch with a degree of latitude for the president to make unilateral decisions.

Justification: This viewpoint is considered conservative as it often hinges on traditional interpretations of the Constitution and a preference for established norms of executive authority. Conservatives may argue that a robust executive branch, led by a decisive president, is essential for effective governance, especially in times of crisis. This perspective values historical precedents where presidential strength was crucial for national security and stability. It reflects a conservative ideology that emphasizes the preservation of certain traditions and structures within government, arguing that these have been proven effective over time and should be maintained to ensure continuity and stability in governance.

Political Analysis

Progressive/Liberal (Left) Viewpoints:

In Support of Stricter Limits on Presidential Power (Progressive Aspect): A significant segment of the left likely holds this view, as it aligns with progressive ideals of checks and balances and preventing authoritarianism. This group may believe in a modern interpretation of the Constitution that evolves with societal changes. Estimated percentage: 70%.

In Support of a Strong Executive Branch (Conservative Aspect): A smaller portion of the left might support this, possibly believing in the efficiency and decisiveness a strong president can bring, especially in crisis situations. This group might prioritize effective governance over strict adherence to checks and balances. Estimated percentage: 30%.

Conservative/Republican (Right) Viewpoints:

In Support of Stricter Limits on Presidential Power (Progressive Aspect): A minority within the conservative camp might align with this perspective, perhaps out of concern for preserving the constitutional balance of power or avoiding potential overreach by the executive branch. Estimated percentage: 25%.

In Support of a Strong Executive Branch (Conservative Aspect): The majority of conservatives likely support this view, valuing traditional interpretations of the Constitution that emphasize a powerful executive for effective governance and national stability, especially in critical times. Estimated percentage: 75%.

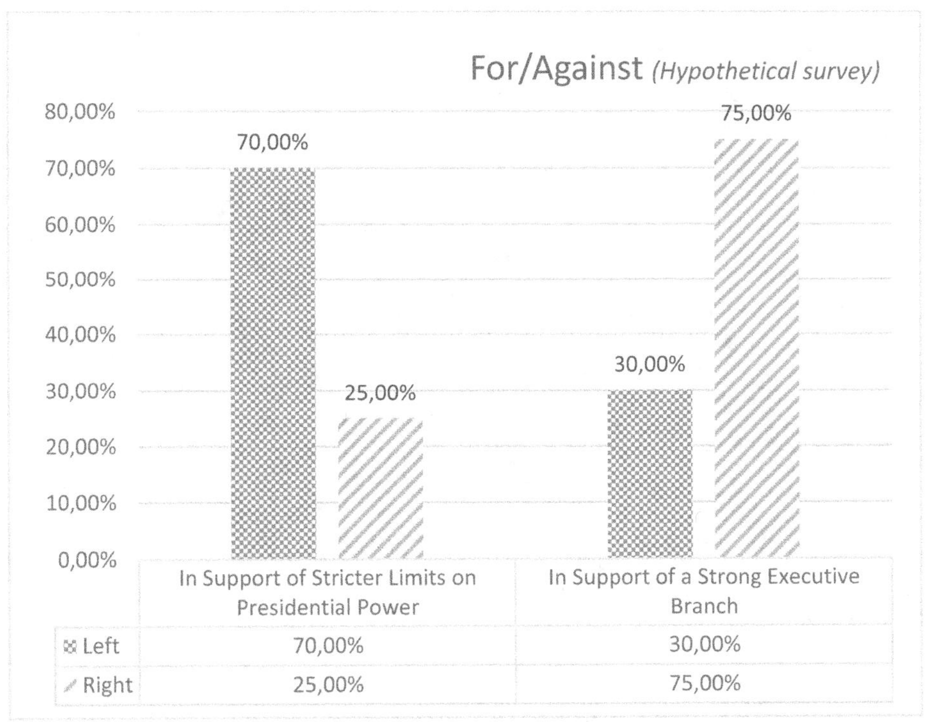

	In Support of Stricter Limits on Presidential Power	In Support of a Strong Executive Branch
Left	70,00%	30,00%
Right	25,00%	75,00%

To Know

Checks in Action: Examples of checks and balances in operation include the president's role as commander-in-chief, countered by Congress's control over military funding and war declarations; Congress's 'power of the purse'; the Senate's role in confirming presidential nominations; and the ability of each house of Congress to check the other. Additionally, the president's veto power and Congress's ability to override vetoes exemplify this balance.[13]

---

[13] https://www.history.com/topics/us-government-and-politics/checks-and-balances

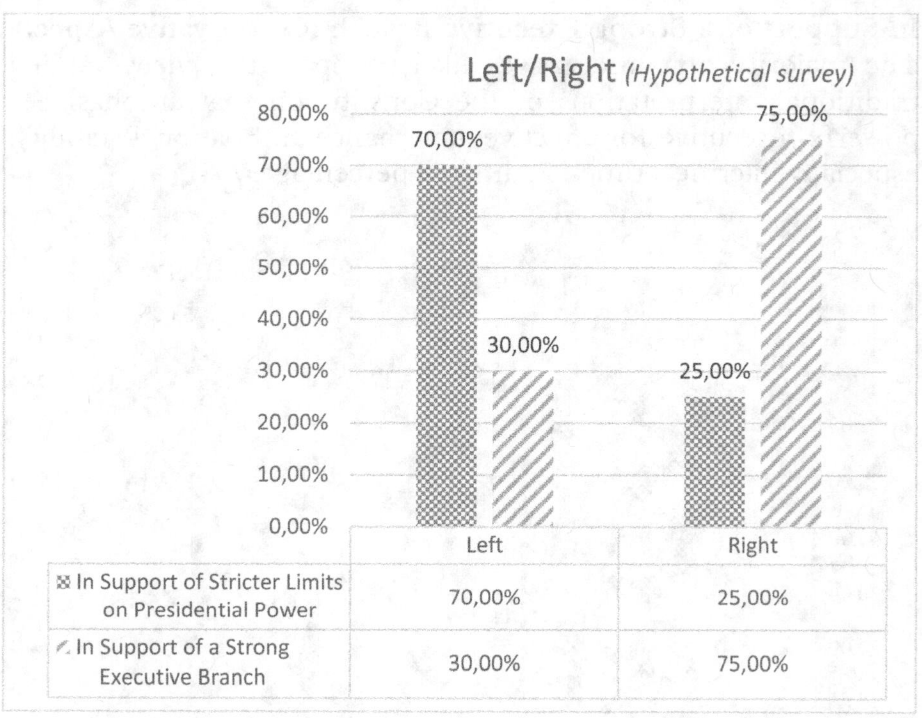

	Left	Right
In Support of Stricter Limits on Presidential Power	70,00%	25,00%
In Support of a Strong Executive Branch	30,00%	75,00%

Motions of the debate

Coalition's Motion (Progressive Viewpoint):

"This house supports the implementation of stringent checks and balances on presidential authority to prevent overreach and safeguard democratic accountability."

Opposition's Motion (Conservative Viewpoint):

"This house opposes restrictions that undermine the effectiveness of the executive branch, asserting the importance of a strong presidential authority for decisive governance and national stability."

Coalition Speech

Ladies and gentlemen, esteemed members of this august gathering,

Today, we stand at a crossroads in the history of our democratic governance. We are here to discuss not just a policy or a rule, but the very essence of our democracy - the balance of power. The motion before us, advocating for stringent checks and balances on presidential authority, is not just a statement, it's a safeguard – a safeguard against the erosion of our most cherished democratic values.

Picture this: A world where leaders turn into rulers, where checks and balances are mere words in dusty books. History has shown us this grim reality time and again. Authoritarian regimes didn't emerge overnight; they sprouted from the seeds of unchecked power. Look back at the 20th century – the rise of dictatorships in Europe. These were not sudden eruptions, but the culmination of power concentrating in the hands of a few, with no checks to hold them back. Our very own Constitution was crafted by visionaries who foresaw this danger. They envisaged a balance, a system where no single branch could overstep its bounds. It's this visionary wisdom we must uphold.

Now, let's talk about accountability, the cornerstone of any democracy. A robust system of checks and balances doesn't just prevent overreach; it ensures that those in power remain answerable to the people. When legislative oversight is effective, it prevents missteps that can have far-reaching consequences. Public trust isn't handed on a silver platter; it's earned, and the best way to earn it is through transparency and accountability. Surveys and studies have consistently shown that public trust in government is higher when there's a perception that power is not concentrated but distributed and monitored.

But let's not be mistaken, advocating for checks and balances isn't advocating for weakness; it's advocating for adaptability and moderation. The challenges we face today – be they economic, social, or technological – require a collaborative approach. A presidency, unrestrained, can lead to policies swinging to extremes, causing more harm than good. We've seen the stability that comes with balanced power, both at home and in other nations.

In conclusion, the motion before us isn't just a choice; it's a responsibility. It's about protecting our future from the mistakes of the past. It's about ensuring that our democracy remains vibrant and true to its founding principles. This house must support stringent checks and balances on presidential power because, at the end of the day, it's about preserving the very essence of what we stand for — a government of the people, by the people, for the people.

Thank you.

Summary of the coalition's arguments

I. Protection Against Authoritarianism
A. Historical Precedence: Authoritarian regimes often start with executive overreach.
- Example: The rise of dictatorships in 20th-century Europe.
- Case Study: Historical instances where unchecked executive power led to erosion of democratic institutions.
B. Constitutional Integrity: The U.S. Constitution envisages a balance of power to prevent tyranny.
- Analysis: Federalist Papers' advocacy for separation of powers.
- Comparison: Different countries' experiences with executive overreach.
II. Ensuring Democratic Accountability
A. Checks and Balances: A strong system of checks and balances is fundamental to democracy.
- Example: Effective legislative oversight in preventing executive missteps.
- Study: Impact of legislative oversight on executive decision-making.
B. Public Trust and Transparency: Limiting presidential power enhances public trust and governmental transparency.
- Survey Data: Public opinion on presidential power and trust in government.
- Case Study: Incidents where transparency prevented misuse of power.
III. Adaptability to Contemporary Challenges
A. Modern Governance Needs: Contemporary challenges require an adaptable approach to presidential powers.
- Analysis: Evolving threats like cyber security and how they're best handled with collaborative governance.

- Example: Success stories of countries with balanced executive-legislative relations addressing modern issues.
B. Preventing Policy Extremism: Balanced power prevents policy swings and extremism.
- Historical Analysis: Instances where unchecked executive power led to extreme policies.
- Comparative Politics: Stability in countries with strong legislative oversight.

Opposition Speech

Ladies and gentlemen, esteemed delegates,

We gather here to debate a matter of great importance - the balance of power in our government, a subject that forms the bedrock of our democracy. However, as we delve into this debate, it is crucial to remember that while checks and balances are essential, they must not come at the cost of paralyzing our government's ability to act decisively and effectively, particularly in times of crisis.

Let us begin by considering the essence of crisis management. History has repeatedly shown that during critical moments, be it war, economic turmoil, or national emergencies, a strong and decisive executive is not just beneficial but necessary. Reflect upon our own history, where prompt presidential decisions have navigated us through dire straits. A strong executive branch, therefore, is not a threat to democracy, but rather a pillar of its effective function.

But this is not just about emergencies. The vision of our founding fathers was of a balanced yet robust executive power. They understood that for a nation to thrive, it needs a leader with the authority to act. This vision is enshrined in our Constitution and has been the guiding principle behind some of the most progressive periods in our history. It is when our presidents have wielded their power effectively that we have seen landmark policies for social and economic betterment.

Moreover, consider the role of the United States on the global stage. In an increasingly complex world, where our leadership is often the bulwark against chaos, a strong executive is imperative. It is presidential decisiveness that has often shaped international relations, brokered peace, and upheld global stability.

Now, let us address the coalition's concerns. Checks and balances are indeed the backbone of our democracy, but let us not confuse oversight with obstruction. The need of the hour is not to limit presidential power, but to ensure it is exercised judiciously and for the public good.

In closing, I urge you to consider the weight of history, the demands of the present, and the vision for our future. A strong, effective executive branch, operating within the bounds of our Constitution, is not just desirable but necessary for the prosperity and stability of our nation.

Thank you.

Summary of the opposition's arguments

I. Necessity of Decisive Leadership
A. Efficiency in Crisis Management: A strong executive can respond more quickly and effectively in emergencies.
- Example: Prompt decision-making during national security threats.
- Case Study: Success of decisive executive actions in historical crises.
B. Unified Policy Direction: A strong president can provide a clear, consistent policy direction.
- Analysis: Fragmented policy making in systems with weak executives.
- Example: Economic or foreign policy successes under strong presidential leadership.
II. Historical and Constitutional Foundations
A. Founders' Vision of Executive Power: The U.S. Constitution envisions a robust executive role.
- Historical Analysis: Interpretations of the Constitution advocating for a strong presidency.
- Example: Founding Fathers' intentions for executive effectiveness and balance.
B. Historical Precedents of Strong Presidencies: Many successful periods in U.S. history were under strong presidential leadership.

- Case Study: Progressive changes under strong presidencies.
- Comparative Analysis: Periods of weak presidencies and associated challenges.
III. Stability and International Standing
A. National Stability: A strong executive contributes to national stability and continuity.
- Comparative Politics: Nations with strong executives and their internal stability.
- Historical Example: Times of turmoil alleviated by decisive presidential action.
B. Global Leadership: A commanding executive presence enhances a country's standing on the world stage.
- International Relations Case Study: Influence of strong U.S. leadership in global affairs.
- Example: Impact of presidential leadership on international agreements and diplomacy.

10 questions from the coalition to the opposition:

1. How can you ensure that a strong executive branch will not lead to the erosion of democratic principles over time?

2. In what ways do you propose to balance decisive presidential action with the necessary legislative oversight to prevent potential abuses of power?

3. What mechanisms would you suggest to ensure that a strong president remains accountable to the electorate and not just to their own agendas?

4. How do you address the historical instances where excessive executive power has led to undemocratic outcomes, even in established democracies?

5. Can you provide examples where increased presidential power has directly resulted in significant and unambiguous benefits for the majority of citizens, rather than select groups or interests?

6. How would a strong executive branch effectively incorporate diverse viewpoints and interests, which is a fundamental aspect of a healthy democracy?

7. What safeguards do you envision to prevent a strong presidency from overshadowing or undermining the other branches of government, thus disrupting the balance of power?

8. How do you reconcile the need for a strong executive with the risk of policy-making becoming overly centralized, potentially ignoring local or minority concerns?

9. In instances where rapid executive decisions have been necessary, how can these decisions be retrospectively scrutinized to ensure they align with democratic values and principles?

10. How do you propose to maintain public trust and transparency in a system where the executive holds significant power and the potential for unilateral decision-making?

10 questions from the opposition to the coalition:

1. How do you propose to handle situations where swift and decisive executive action is necessary but legislative processes are inherently slow?

2. What measures would you suggest to prevent legislative overreach and ensure that checks and balances do not turn into legislative obstructionism?

3. How can a system with stringent checks on presidential power avoid becoming ineffective, especially in dealing with urgent and unforeseen national crises?

4. Can you provide historical examples where increased legislative oversight directly resulted in better governance and outcomes for the general populace?

5. How do you address the risk of political gridlock that can arise from overly stringent checks on executive power, potentially hindering effective governance?

6. In your model of increased checks and balances, how do you ensure that the executive branch retains enough authority to fulfill its constitutional responsibilities effectively?

7. What mechanisms would you implement to ensure that the legislative branch's oversight of the executive does not become politicized and used as a tool for political rivalry?

8. How do you propose to balance the need for transparency and accountability with the need for confidentiality in certain aspects of national security and international diplomacy?

9. How would your approach encourage the executive branch to take necessary risks and innovative approaches in policy-making, which might be hindered by fear of over-scrutiny?

10. In cases where rapid response to international events is crucial, how do you envision the executive and legislative branches working together without the delays that might arise from increased checks?

Potential solutions to reconcile the two parties

In the intricate dance of governance, where the rhythm of democracy is set by the delicate balance between executive decisiveness and legislative oversight, finding common ground is not just desirable, it's essential for the health of our nation. Let us embark on a journey to explore potential solutions and compromises that respect the viewpoints of both the coalition and the opposition, weaving a tapestry of mutual understanding and agreement.

Our first step lies in the **establishment of a bipartisan oversight committee**. This committee, representative of both parties, would serve as a check on presidential power, ensuring that decisions are made in the nation's best interest, not just the executive's. But this is not enough. To prevent legislative overreach and maintain an effective executive branch, we must also consider **implementing clear guidelines** that define the limits of this oversight, ensuring it remains constructive, not obstructive.

In times of crisis, when swift action is paramount, we could establish a protocol for **expedited legislative review**. This approach respects the necessity of quick executive action while maintaining a degree of legislative oversight. Furthermore, to balance this fast-tracking process, there could be a **post-decision review mechanism**, ensuring accountability and transparency, even in retrospect.

The next step in our journey is to **enhance transparency** in executive decision-making. This could be achieved through regular reports to Congress, offering a window into the executive's reasoning and actions. However, to respect the confidentiality required in certain areas, especially national security, we must agree on **specific parameters** that define what information must be shared and what can remain confidential.

Addressing the concern of political gridlock, our path leads us to **mediation mechanisms** within Congress, designed to resolve disputes and ensure efficient governance. This solution respects the need for checks and balances while mitigating the risk of legislative obstructionism.

To ensure that the executive branch retains its necessary authority, we must also look at **streamlining legislative processes**, making them more efficient and less prone to causing unnecessary delays in policy implementation.

As we near the end of our journey, we find ourselves contemplating the importance of **public involvement and feedback**. Establishing regular town halls or forums where citizens can voice their concerns and suggestions could bridge the gap between government actions and public sentiment.

Finally, we arrive at the need for **continuous review and adaptation** of these measures. Regular assessments of the effectiveness of these solutions would ensure that they remain relevant and effective in the ever-evolving landscape of our democratic governance.

In this journey, we have explored avenues that respect the need for a strong, decisive executive and the imperative of robust legislative oversight. Through these solutions, we seek not just compromise, but a harmonious balance that upholds the spirit of our democracy.

Recommended Resources

Checks in the Balance: Legislative Capacity and the Dynamics of Executive Power[14] by Alexander Bolton and Sharece Thrower

Coalition/Opposition Breakdown: 60/40

This book presents a new theory of separation of powers that emphasizes the importance of legislative capacity in constraining presidential and gubernatorial power. While it acknowledges the significance of executive power, its main focus is on empowering legislatures to effectively check ambitious executives. This slightly favors the coalition's viewpoint of advocating for checks and balances but also recognizes the role of executive power, hence the 60/40 breakdown.

By Executive Order: Bureaucratic Management and the Limits of Presidential Power[15] by Andrew Rudalevige

Coalition/Opposition Breakdown: 40/60

The book delves into the common perception of the U.S. president wielding extraordinary personal power through executive orders, clarifying that most such orders are proposed by federal agencies and shaped by negotiations within the executive branch. This perspective leans more towards the opposition's viewpoint, emphasizing the complexity and collaborative nature of executive power rather than solely viewing it as unilateral presidential authority. However, it does not fully align with the opposition's stance as it acknowledges the checks within the executive branch itself, thus the 40/60 breakdown.

---

[14] https://amzn.to/3NsXiBT
[15] https://amzn.to/3taGwR4

Presidential Power and the Modern Presidents: The Politics of Leadership from Roosevelt to Reagan[16] by Richard E. Neustadt

Coalition/Opposition Breakdown: 30/70

The book focuses on presidential power and leadership. It emphasizes the importance and effectiveness of presidential leadership, aligning more with the opposition's stance on the need for a strong executive.

Investigating the President: Congressional Checks on Presidential Power[17] by Douglas Kriner and Eric Schickler

Coalition/Opposition Breakdown: 70/30

This book presents a comprehensive overview of congressional investigative oversight and its role as a powerful tool for Congress to counter presidential aggrandizement. By highlighting the effectiveness of congressional investigations in exerting significant pressure on the president and affecting policy outcomes, it aligns more with the coalition's viewpoint on the need for checks and balances. However, it also acknowledges the complexities of these investigations, which prevents it from being entirely one-sided, leading to a 70/30 breakdown.

---

[16] https://amzn.to/41lNxuW
[17] https://amzn.to/3v0rMVv

Chapter 5: The Influence of Social Media on Political Mobilization and Radicalization

Discussing the role of social media platforms in fueling political extremism.

The most polarizing aspect of the influence of social media on political mobilization and radicalization lies in the debate over the extent of responsibility and power social media platforms have in fueling political extremism. This contentious point revolves around the question of whether social media acts merely as a mirror reflecting pre-existing societal divisions or as an active catalyst that exacerbates and intensifies political radicalization.

On one side of the debate, there is a strong argument that social media platforms, with their algorithms designed to maximize engagement, inadvertently promote extreme content. These algorithms, critics argue, create echo chambers and filter bubbles, where users are continuously exposed to more radical views, reinforcing their existing beliefs and pushing them further towards extremism. This perspective holds that social media platforms are not just passive players but have an active role in shaping political discourse, often to the detriment of moderate, balanced viewpoints.

Contrastingly, another viewpoint asserts that social media is simply a tool, a reflection of the broader society, and that the root causes of radicalization lie elsewhere – in economic, social, and political conditions. Proponents of this view argue that blaming social media oversimplifies complex societal issues and diverts attention from more fundamental causes of extremism, such as systemic inequality, political disenfranchisement, or cultural conflicts. They contend that while social media can amplify voices, it does not inherently generate extremist ideologies.

This debate is intensely polarizing because it touches on fundamental issues of free speech, censorship, and the role of technology in society. The heart of the contention lies in balancing the need to protect democratic discourse and prevent radicalization, against preserving the openness and freedom that are intrinsic to social media. It raises critical questions about the extent to which technology companies should be responsible for monitoring and regulating content, and the potential implications of such regulation on free expression and privacy.

The strength of the disagreement comes from the high stakes involved: the integrity of political processes, the health of public discourse, and the preservation of democratic values. As social media continues to be an integral part of our daily lives, this debate remains at the forefront, reflecting deep societal anxieties about technology, power, and the nature of democracy itself.

Progressive and Conservative Viewpoints:

Identify the Progressive Viewpoint:

Aspect: The argument that social media platforms have a responsibility to actively monitor and regulate content to prevent political extremism.

Justification: This aspect is considered progressive due to its emphasis on change and adaptation in the face of new challenges posed by technology. It aligns with progressive ideologies that advocate for active intervention and reform to address societal issues. The viewpoint reflects a modern interpretation of the role of technology in society, prioritizing the need to adapt regulations and oversight to new forms of media. It also involves a concern for greater social equality and the prevention of harm, as it seeks to mitigate the spread of extreme, divisive content that could exacerbate social and political inequalities.

Identify the Conservative Viewpoint:

Aspect: The belief that social media is merely a reflection of existing societal divisions and that the root causes of radicalization lie in traditional societal structures rather than the platforms themselves.

Justification: This aspect is considered conservative as it emphasizes the importance of historical context and the preservation of established norms, particularly regarding free speech and the role of private companies in regulating content. It suggests a cautious approach to changing the status quo, focusing on the fundamental causes of extremism rather than the tools (like social media) through which they manifest. This viewpoint aligns with conservative ideologies that prioritize individual responsibility over systemic intervention and caution against extensive regulation that might impede free market principles or freedom of expression.

Political Analysis

Progressive/Liberal (Left) Viewpoints:

In Support of Active Regulation by Social Media Platforms (Progressive Aspect of the Topic): A significant segment of the left views the proactive regulation of content on social media platforms as essential for combating political extremism and misinformation. They believe these platforms have a responsibility to prevent the spread of harmful content that can lead to radicalization and societal division. This group, which may include activists, technology critics, and those concerned about the impact of social media on democracy, could represent approximately 70% of the progressive viewpoint.

In Support of Social Media Reflecting Societal Divisions (Conservative Aspect of the Topic): A smaller portion of the left might support the idea that social media is a mirror of existing societal issues rather than a catalyst. They could argue that focusing too much on social media diverts attention from addressing deeper societal problems like inequality and political disenfranchisement. This viewpoint, potentially held by civil libertarians and free speech advocates within the progressive camp, might constitute about 30% of the liberal perspective.

Conservative/Republican (Right) Viewpoints:

In Support of Active Regulation by Social Media Platforms (Progressive Aspect of the Topic): A minority within the conservative spectrum may agree with the need for some level of regulation by social media platforms, perhaps due to concerns about national security, the spread of extremist ideologies, or the preservation of social order. This group might represent about 25% of the conservative viewpoint.

In Support of Social Media Reflecting Societal Divisions (Conservative Aspect of the Topic): The majority of conservatives likely align with the view that social media platforms are merely reflecting pre-existing societal divisions. This group, emphasizing free speech and minimal regulatory interference in private enterprises, might argue that the root causes of extremism are more complex and not primarily the responsibility of technology platforms. This perspective, favoring traditional values and skeptical of increased regulation, could comprise around 75% of the right-leaning viewpoint.

To Know

While social media is commonly thought to drive polarization, its impact appears more nuanced than initially believed. Social media platforms like Facebook, Reddit, and Twitter amplify moral and emotional messages, organizing users into digital communities often based on tribal conflicts. However, the degree to which this contributes to overall political polarization is subtler than direct causation.[18]

---

[18]

https://greatergood.berkeley.edu/article/item/is_social_media_driving_political_polarization

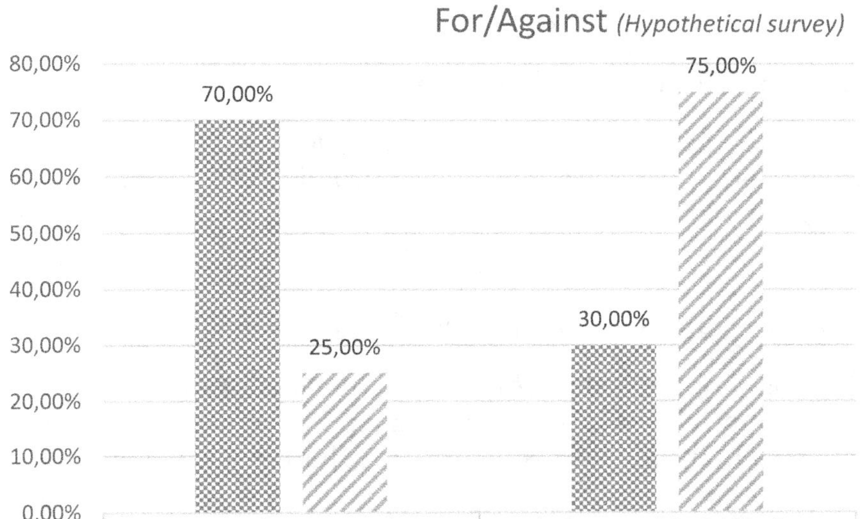

For/Against *(Hypothetical survey)*

	In Support of Active Regulation by Social Media Platforms	In Support of Social Media Reflecting Societal Divisions
Left	70,00%	30,00%
Right	25,00%	75,00%

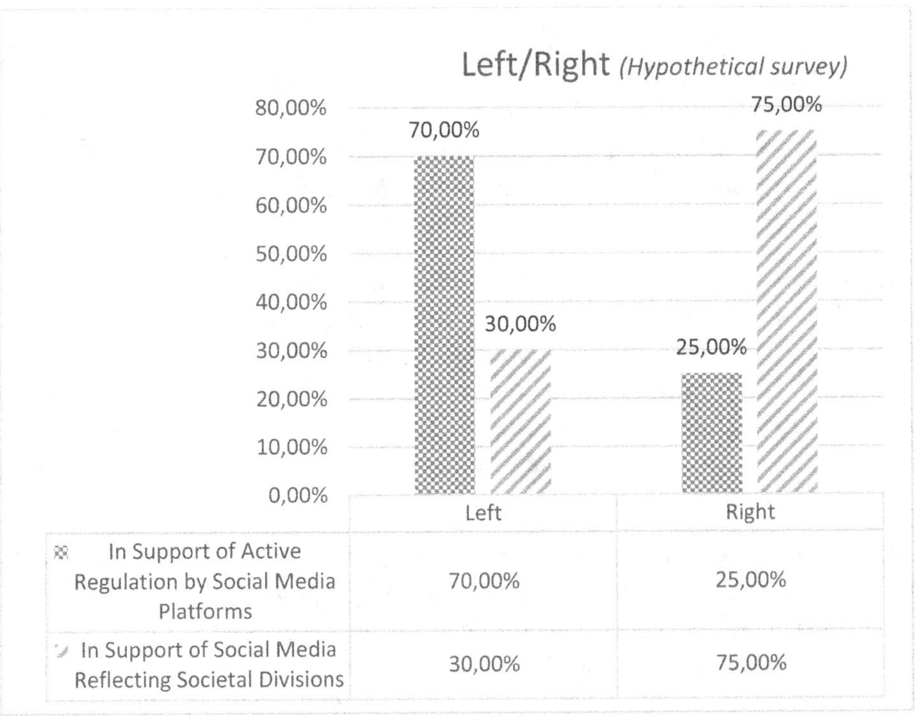

Left/Right *(Hypothetical survey)*

	Left	Right
In Support of Active Regulation by Social Media Platforms	70,00%	25,00%
In Support of Social Media Reflecting Societal Divisions	30,00%	75,00%

Motions of the debate

Coalition's Motion (Progressive Viewpoint):

"This house supports the active regulation of content on social media platforms to combat political extremism and misinformation."

Opposition's Motion (Conservative Viewpoint):

"This house opposes the idea that social media platforms should be held responsible for political radicalization, and believes that the focus should be on addressing the underlying societal issues."

Coalition Speech

Ladies and Gentlemen,

In this age of information, where social media has become the town square of our digital era, we stand at a crossroads. Today, I speak to you not just as a debater, but as a citizen deeply concerned about the fabric of our society. I stand before you to argue passionately in favor of the motion that social media platforms must take active responsibility for regulating content to combat political extremism and misinformation.

Let us begin by peering into the heart of social media - its algorithms. These invisible codes, designed to captivate and engage, often become unwitting accomplices in amplifying extremist content. Think of the countless instances where misinformation spread like wildfire, igniting real-world consequences. These algorithms, in their quest for engagement, create echo chambers, isolating us from diverse viewpoints and reinforcing our existing beliefs.

But the issue runs deeper, touching the very core of our democratic processes. Consider how misinformation and targeted propaganda on social media have influenced elections worldwide. Can we forget the instances where foreign entities used these platforms to sow discord in our political landscapes? Social media, unchecked, poses a risk to the very quality of our public discourse, giving rise to conspiracy theories that have led to violence and public harm.

Yet, our argument goes beyond just the protection of democratic processes. It's about the fabric of our social harmony. We have witnessed the correlation between online hate speech and incidents of communal violence. The regulation of extreme content has, in some cases, led to a decrease in hate crimes. This is not just about algorithms and engagement; it's about preserving the values of decency and respect in our society.

So, as we navigate these complex waters, let us ask ourselves: Can we afford to let social media platforms remain unchecked, to let these algorithms run wild? Can we stand idly by while our public discourse is hijacked by the loudest and most extreme voices?

The answer, ladies and gentlemen, is a resounding no. The time for action is now. It's time for social media platforms to step up and take responsibility for the content they disseminate. It's time to protect our democratic discourse, our societal harmony, and the values we hold dear.

In conclusion, let us not look back at this moment in history and wish we had done more. Let us be the architects of a future where social media is a force for good, a platform for healthy, democratic discourse. Let's support this motion, not just for ourselves, but for future generations.

Thank you.

Summary of the coalition's arguments

I. Responsibility of Social Media Platforms
A. Algorithmic Amplification of Extremist Content
- Studies show algorithms used by social media platforms often prioritize and amplify extreme content because it generates more engagement.
- Incidents where misinformation or radical ideologies went viral, leading to real-world consequences.
B. Creation of Echo Chambers
- Research indicates that social media algorithms create echo chambers, isolating users from diverse viewpoints and reinforcing existing beliefs.

- Examples of social media groups that became radicalized due to exposure to a narrow range of extremist opinions.
II. Protection of Democratic Processes
A. Influence on Public Opinion and Elections
- Evidence from elections worldwide showing how misinformation and targeted propaganda on social media can influence voter behavior.
- Instances where foreign entities used social media to disseminate divisive content, impacting national politics.
B. Risks to Public Discourse
- Analysis of how extreme content on social media polarizes public discourse, undermining the quality of democratic debate.
- Examples of social media-driven conspiracy theories that led to public harm or violence.
III. Preventive Measures for Social Harmony
A. Reducing the Spread of Hate Speech and Violence
- Data showing a correlation between online hate speech and incidents of communal violence.
- Success stories where regulation of extreme content led to a decrease in hate crimes.
B. Upholding Societal Values
- Argument for social media reflecting societal norms of decency and respect, not just profitability.
- Cases where social media intervention prevented the spread of dangerous ideologies.

Opposition Speech

Ladies and gentlemen, esteemed members of the audience,

Today, I stand before you to challenge a prevailing notion that is as dangerous as it is misleading: the idea that social media platforms should bear the brunt of responsibility for political radicalization. This motion, while well-intentioned, overlooks the fundamental principles of freedom and the complex nature of radicalization itself.

Let us first address the elephant in the room: freedom of speech and expression. The path this motion leads us down is fraught with censorship and suppression. To give social media platforms the power to regulate content is to hand them the keys to control political discourse. History is replete with examples where control over media led to authoritarian regimes stifling opposition under the guise of protecting the public.

But let's delve deeper. The core argument of the coalition hinges on the assumption that social media is the primary catalyst for radicalization. This is a simplistic view that ignores the multifaceted nature of this process. Radicalization is rooted in a complex interplay of societal issues, often born out of economic, social, and political strife. By focusing solely on social media, we risk neglecting these underlying causes.

Moreover, the inefficacy of platform regulation cannot be overstated. When one door closes, another opens. Extremism, if pushed off mainstream platforms, will find new homes, perhaps less visible but more dangerous. This is not a solution, but a displacement of the problem.

Now, consider the potential negative consequences of such regulation. Innovation and the growth of social media platforms are at stake. Overregulation can stifle the very essence of these platforms, hindering technological advancement and economic growth. And let's not forget the privacy and autonomy of users, which stand to be violated in the pursuit of invasive monitoring.

So, where does this leave us? The answer does not lie in handing over the reins of control to social media platforms but in addressing the root causes of radicalization. It lies in fostering open, democratic discourse, not in curtailing it.

In conclusion, I urge you to consider the implications of supporting this motion. Let us not trade our freedoms for a false sense of security. Let us tackle radicalization at its roots, rather than trimming its digital branches.

Thank you.

Summary of the opposition's arguments

I. Freedom of Speech and Expression
A. Censorship Concerns
- Highlighting how excessive regulation of social media can lead to censorship and suppression of free speech.
- Examples of social media platforms erroneously censoring legitimate political discourse in the name of controlling extremism.
B. Slippery Slope to Authoritarian Control
- The risk of setting a precedent that could be exploited by governments to suppress dissent and control public opinion.
- Historical instances where control over media was used by authoritarian regimes to stifle opposition.
II. Ineffectiveness and Misdirection of Blame
A. Complexity of Radicalization
- Evidence showing that radicalization is a multifaceted process influenced more by offline factors than social media.
- Case studies of individuals radicalized without significant online influence, pointing to deeper societal issues.
B. Inefficacy of Platform Regulation
- Studies indicating that regulation on one platform simply pushes extremist content to less regulated or new platforms.
- Instances where regulation failed to curb the spread of extremism but stifled meaningful dialogue.
III. Potential Negative Consequences of Regulation
A. Impact on Innovation and Growth
- How stringent regulation can stifle innovation and the growth of social media platforms, negatively impacting the economy.
- Examples of technological advancements slowed or halted due to overregulation.
B. Violation of User Privacy and Autonomy
- The invasive monitoring required for regulation leading to privacy concerns and violation of personal autonomy.
- Incidents where data collected for regulation was misused or mishandled.

1. How can you reconcile the need for freedom of speech with the responsibility to prevent the spread of harmful misinformation that can lead to real-world violence?

2. What mechanisms would you propose to address the issue of social media being used by foreign entities to interfere in democratic processes, if not through regulation?

3. Can you provide examples of effective alternative strategies that have been successful in curbing online radicalization without infringing on freedom of speech?

4. How does your argument account for the fact that social media algorithms are designed to promote engagement, often leading to the amplification of extreme content?

5. In what ways do you suggest society tackle the echo chambers created by social media that contribute to political polarization, if not through platform regulation?

6. Given the global reach of social media platforms, how would you suggest they address the issue of hate speech that crosses cultural and national boundaries without some form of content control?

7. How would you respond to the argument that inaction by social media platforms in regulating content is a form of tacit endorsement or complicity in the spread of extremist ideologies?

8. Considering the rapid evolution of digital communication, how do you propose to ensure that the principles of free speech are upheld without allowing the unchecked spread of misinformation and extremist rhetoric?

9. Can you elaborate on how the right to free speech should be balanced with the need to protect vulnerable communities from targeted hate speech and misinformation campaigns?

10. If radicalization is primarily rooted in offline societal issues, how do you explain the accelerated rate of radicalization observed in individuals who are heavily influenced by extremist content on social media platforms?

1. How do you propose social media platforms distinguish between harmful misinformation and legitimate political discourse without infringing on free speech rights?

2. What specific criteria would you suggest for social media platforms to use in identifying and regulating extremist content, given the subjective nature of such judgments?

3. Can you provide evidence that regulating content on social media platforms directly leads to a decrease in real-world political extremism and violence?

4. How would you address concerns that increased regulation on social media could lead to a chilling effect on free expression, particularly among marginalized and dissenting voices?

5. In what ways do you plan to ensure that the power to regulate content does not become a tool for political or ideological censorship by either the platforms or governments?

6. How would the coalition's proposed regulations adapt to the constantly evolving landscape of digital communication and social media platforms?

7. Can you cite examples from history where similar regulation of communication mediums successfully balanced the protection of public discourse without overreaching into censorship?

8. How do you propose to safeguard the rights of users against potential misuse of data collected during the monitoring and regulation process by social media companies?

9. What measures would you suggest to prevent the regulatory burden from stifling innovation and competition among social media platforms?

10. Given the global nature of social media, how do you plan to reconcile differing national standards and cultural norms regarding free speech and acceptable content within your regulatory framework?

Potential solutions to reconcile the two parties

In seeking a resolution to the complex debate surrounding the role of social media in political mobilization and radicalization, it's vital to find common ground that honors the concerns of both the coalition advocating for regulation and the opposition wary of censorship and free speech infringement.

A starting point could be the **development of transparent content moderation policies**, with clear guidelines that balance the need to curb harmful content while protecting free speech. This approach respects the coalition's call for responsible content management while addressing the opposition's fear of arbitrary censorship. To further this goal, the implementation of an **independent oversight board** comprising experts from various fields, including human rights, technology, and law, could ensure fair and unbiased decision-making.

Recognizing the coalition's concerns about algorithmic amplification of extremist content, a compromise might involve **adjusting algorithms to reduce echo chambers**, yet doing so transparently and under external review to safeguard against potential biases. This step would demonstrate a commitment to reducing harmful content's virality without resorting to outright bans or censorship.

To address the opposition's concerns about the effectiveness of regulation, a shared solution could involve **investing in digital literacy programs**. These programs would empower users to critically assess online information, thus tackling the problem of misinformation at its root by fostering a more discerning audience.

Another potential area of agreement is the **enhanced use of AI and machine learning tools** to flag potential extremist content. However, to avoid overreliance on automated systems that may lack nuance, these tools should be complemented by **human moderation**, especially for complex content decisions. This blend respects the coalition's call for proactive measures while considering the opposition's concerns about automated censorship.

Acknowledging the global nature of social media, both sides might agree on the necessity of **international cooperation and standard-setting**. This cooperation could involve sharing best practices and developing global standards for content moderation that reflect a diverse range of perspectives and legal frameworks.

Given the concerns about privacy and data misuse, a mutually acceptable solution could involve **strict data privacy regulations** to protect users' information during the content moderation process. This would reassure users and both sides of the debate about the ethical handling of data.

To ensure ongoing dialogues and continuous improvement, setting up **regular public forums for feedback and discussion** could provide transparency and accountability. These forums would allow stakeholders, including civil society, tech companies, and users, to voice their concerns and suggestions, fostering a sense of community involvement in decision-making.

A key compromise could also involve **periodic review and adaptation of policies**, ensuring that content moderation strategies evolve in line with technological advancements and societal changes. This dynamic approach would help maintain a balance between protecting public discourse and upholding freedom of expression.

Lastly, the establishment of a **mechanism for appeal and redress** for users who feel their content was unfairly moderated could build trust and offer a safeguard against potential misuse of moderation powers.

Through these carefully considered compromises, it's possible to construct a framework that respects the importance of free speech and the need to protect society from the harms of unchecked extremist content, paving the way for a more balanced and effective approach to managing social media's complex role in modern politics.

Recommended Resources

Breaking the Social Media Prism: How to Make Our Platforms Less Polarizing[19] by Chris Bail

Coalition/Opposition Breakdown: 40/60

Chris Bail's work suggests that while social media platforms do play a role in political polarization, the more significant factors are human nature, our search for identity, and status. This leans slightly more towards the opposition's viewpoint, as it downplays the direct influence of social media platforms in favor of broader human behavioral factors.

Frenemies: How Social Media Polarizes America by Jaime Settle

Coalition/Opposition Breakdown: 50/50

Jaime Settle's book provides a balanced examination of how social media contributes to political polarization. It introduces the END Framework, which analyzes how social media interactions can lead to negative attitudes towards political out-groups. This book treats the subject neutrally by acknowledging the role of social media in polarization while also considering the inherent features of these platforms and user behavior.

---

[19] https://amzn.to/3thevXR

Chapter 6: Comparative Analysis of Democratic Erosion Globally

Debating similarities and differences between the U.S. political climate and other countries experiencing democratic backsliding.

The heart of the debate in the comparative analysis of democratic erosion globally, particularly when juxtaposing the U.S. political climate with other nations experiencing democratic backsliding, lies in the contentious issue of the role and influence of populist movements and leaders. This aspect has become the focal point of contention due to its profound impact on the traditional democratic processes and institutions.

Populist movements, often characterized by their charismatic leaders, appeal to the general populace by presenting themselves as an alternative to the established political order. They claim to represent the "voice of the people" against what they portray as a corrupt and elitist political establishment. This phenomenon is not unique to the United States; countries across the world have witnessed the rise of such movements, which challenge the status quo and, in some cases, upend longstanding democratic norms and institutions.

The debate intensifies when discussing how these populist movements influence democratic systems. On one side, proponents argue that these movements are a necessary response to the failures of the political elite, offering a corrective measure to re-align politics with the will of the people. They view these movements as revitalizing democracy by bringing forth issues often ignored by mainstream politics and giving a voice to those who feel disenfranchised.

Conversely, critics of populist movements see them as a threat to democratic principles. They argue that while these movements claim to represent the people, they often undermine democratic institutions and norms, such as the independence of the judiciary, freedom of the press, and the protection of minority rights. By centralizing power and often appealing to divisive, nationalist sentiments, these movements, according to critics, can lead to authoritarianism and the erosion of democratic safeguards.

This dichotomy provokes strong debate because it touches on fundamental questions about the nature of democracy itself. It raises concerns about how democracies should respond to popular discontent, the balance between majority rule and the protection of minority rights, and the resilience of democratic institutions in the face of populist challenges. The debate is further complicated by the global nature of this trend, as it forces a comparison between different political cultures and historical contexts, making it a complex and multifaceted issue that continues to be a source of deep division and discussion in the analysis of democratic erosion worldwide.

Progressive and Conservative Viewpoints:

Identify the Progressive Viewpoint:

Aspect: Criticism of Populist Movements

The progressive viewpoint in this debate is aligned with the criticism of populist movements. Progressives often perceive these movements as threats to democratic norms and institutions, such as the independence of the judiciary, freedom of the press, and the rights of minorities.

Justification:

This aspect is considered progressive because it aligns with the ideological emphasis on protecting and advancing civil liberties, human rights, and democratic institutions. Progressives typically advocate for social reform and equality, and they view the centralization of power and nationalist rhetoric often associated with populist movements as contrary to these principles. They argue for the importance of maintaining democratic checks and balances and are wary of any political shift that might undermine these.

Identify the Conservative Viewpoint:

Aspect: Support for Populist Movements

The conservative viewpoint in this context aligns with support for populist movements. Conservatives often view these movements as a necessary correction to the perceived failures of the political elite and a return to what they see as the true representation of the people's will.

Justification:

This aspect is considered conservative as it often involves a preference for maintaining or returning to traditional values and structures. Conservatives might view populist movements as a means to reassert national identity and sovereignty, which they often prioritize. This perspective also tends to emphasize the role of populist movements in challenging and potentially reshaping the existing political order, which conservatives might see as having drifted away from the country's foundational principles or the perceived will of the majority. This viewpoint aligns with conservative ideologies that emphasize the preservation of certain traditions, historical contexts, and the stability of established social norms.

Political Analysis

Progressive/Liberal (Left) Viewpoints:

In Support of Criticism of Populist Movements: A significant portion of the progressive/left spectrum likely aligns with this viewpoint. They might view populist movements as undermining democratic institutions and threatening civil liberties. This group probably represents about 70% of the left-leaning population. They prioritize protecting democratic norms, human rights, and advocating for social reforms.

In Support of Populist Movements: A smaller segment of the left might support certain aspects of populist movements, particularly those that promise social reforms or challenge established political elites perceived as disconnected from the populace. This group, focusing on the potential for systemic change and addressing inequalities, could represent about 30% of the progressive/left spectrum.

Conservative/Republican (Right) Viewpoints:

In Support of Criticism of Populist Movements: Within the conservative/right spectrum, a smaller faction might share concerns about the potential for populist movements to destabilize democratic institutions or erode traditional values. They might also be wary of the authoritarian tendencies within some populist leaders. This group could account for about 20% of the conservative population.

In Support of Populist Movements: The majority of the conservative/right spectrum likely aligns with this viewpoint. They may view populist movements as a corrective to the perceived failures of the political establishment and a way to reaffirm national identity and values. This viewpoint, which sees populist movements as re-aligning politics with the will of the people and preserving traditional norms, might represent about 80% of the conservative population.

To Know

Slow Erosion of Democracies: Democracies in decline typically experience a gradual erosion rather than abrupt changes. This slow process often includes legislative and procedural changes that make voting more challenging, contesting incumbents harder, and turning electoral victory into substantial policy impact more difficult.[20]

---

[20] https://www.brookings.edu/articles/four-things-to-know-about-democratic-erosion/

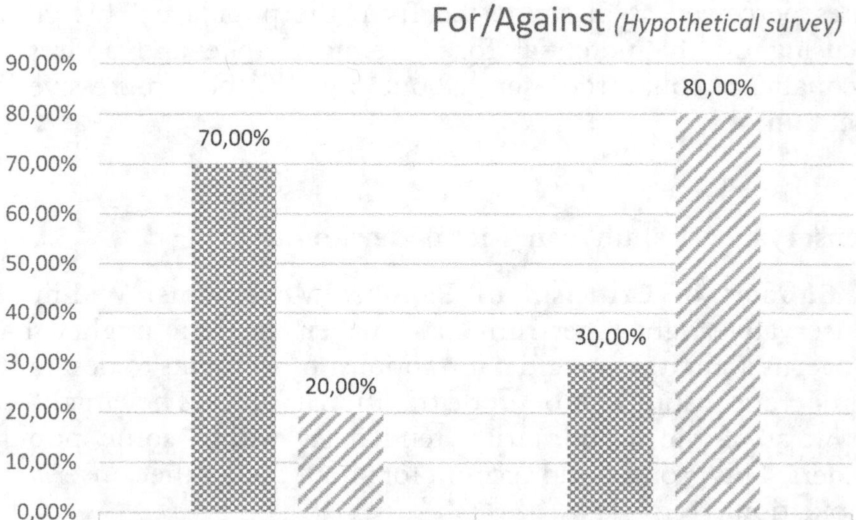

For/Against *(Hypothetical survey)*

	In Support of Criticism of Populist Movements	In Support of Populist Movements
Left	70,00%	30,00%
Right	20,00%	80,00%

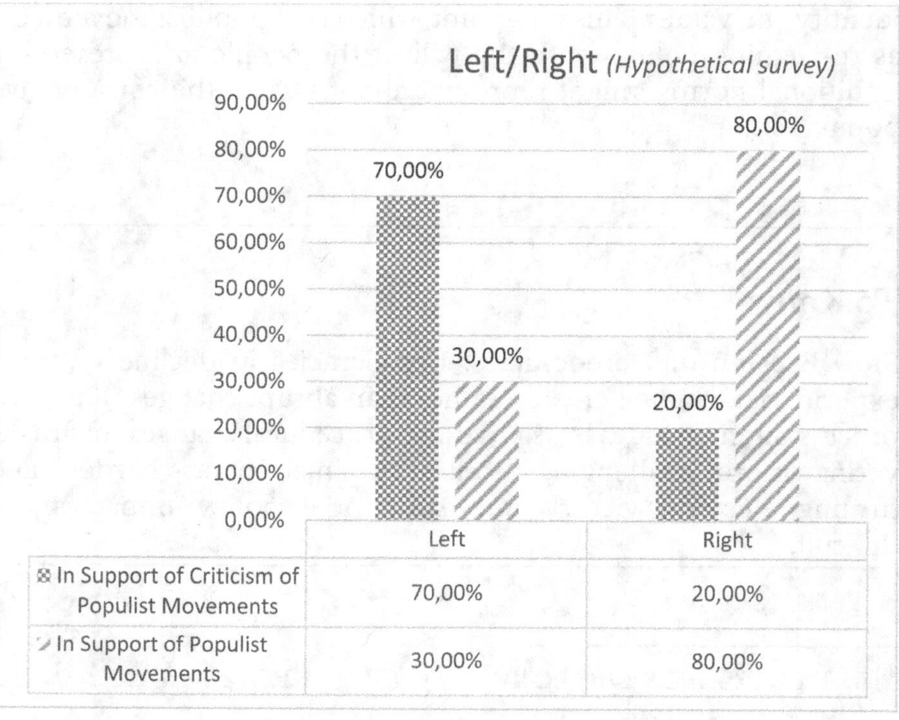

Left/Right *(Hypothetical survey)*

	Left	Right
In Support of Criticism of Populist Movements	70,00%	20,00%
In Support of Populist Movements	30,00%	80,00%

Motions of the debate

Coalition's Motion (Progressive Viewpoint):

"This house supports the strict upholding of democratic norms and institutions against the erosion caused by populist movements."

Opposition's Motion (Conservative Viewpoint):

"This house opposes the characterization of populist movements as threats to democracy, affirming their role in representing the will of the people and correcting political elitism."

Coalition Speech

Ladies and gentlemen, esteemed judges, and fellow debaters, today we stand at a crossroads in history, a moment where the very fabric of our democracies is under scrutiny. We are here to affirm a fundamental truth: that the preservation of democratic norms and institutions is paramount, especially in the face of populist movements that threaten to unravel them.

Picture this: a society where the judiciary, the guardian of our rights, is swayed not by the rule of law, but by the whims of populist rhetoric. A world where the free press, our watchdog against tyranny, is muzzled, leaving the powerful unchecked. This is not a dystopian fantasy, but a possible reality if we do not stand firm in support of our democratic institutions.

Think of the independent judiciary as the cornerstone of our democracy, essential in preventing the dangerous concentration of power. Remember the times when individual rights and freedoms were trampled under the guise of popular sentiment. Recall how a free press has exposed corruption and held leaders accountable, and how its suppression has often been the first step towards authoritarian regimes.

But our argument goes beyond the protection of institutions. It's about the people these institutions serve. It's about ensuring that the voices of all, especially the minorities, are heard and respected. History has shown us, time and again, how populist movements, under the guise of representing the majority, have eroded minority rights, leading to societies where diversity is not celebrated but suppressed.

We must also address the balance between majority rule and minority rights. A true democracy does not just bow to the majority but also safeguards the interests of the minority. The stability and health of a democracy are measured not only by the voice of the majority but also by the protections afforded to the minority.

And let us not forget the slippery slope that leads from populist rhetoric to authoritarian rule. History is replete with examples where leaders, riding the wave of populism, have centralized power, dismantling the very checks and balances that prevent autocratic rule.

Today, we stand for more than just a motion. We stand for the preservation of our democratic way of life. We stand for a world where rights are not granted by the whims of the majority but are inalienable and protected by robust institutions. We stand for a democracy that values every voice, majority and minority alike.

In conclusion, this is not just a debate about policies or politics. It's a debate about our future, the kind of world we want to live in. Do we choose a path that safeguards our democratic institutions, protects our freedoms, and upholds our values? Or do we stray into uncharted waters, risking the very essence of what makes us democratic? The choice is clear. We must support the strict upholding of democratic norms and institutions against the erosion caused by populist movements. Thank you.

Summary of the coalition's arguments

I. Upholding Democratic Institutions
A. Vitality of Independent Judiciary
- Importance in preventing the concentration of power
- Role in safeguarding individual rights and freedoms
B. Necessity of Free Press
- Free press as a watchdog against governmental overreach
- Historical instances where a suppressed press led to authoritarian regimes
II. Protecting Civil Liberties and Minority Rights
A. History of Populism and Minority Rights

- Examples where populist movements have led to the erosion of minority protections
- The necessity of protecting diverse voices in a democracy
B. Balancing Majority Rule and Minority Rights
- The danger of majoritarianism in overriding minority interests
- Democratic stability reliant on respecting and protecting minority opinions
III. Preventing Authoritarianism
A. Slippery Slope of Populist Rhetoric
- Historical examples where populist rhetoric led to authoritarian rule
- The importance of rhetoric in shaping public perception and policy
B. Concentration of Power and Erosion of Checks and Balances
- Instances where populist leaders undermined democratic institutions
- The critical role of checks and balances in preventing autocratic rule

Opposition Speech

Ladies and gentlemen, esteemed judges, and fellow debaters, today we gather to confront a motion that, while well-intentioned, overlooks the fundamental dynamics of democracy. We stand in opposition, not to defend the erosion of democracy, but to advocate for its truest form - a form that echoes the voices of the many, not just the few.

Let us begin by addressing a crucial misconception: populism is not the enemy of democracy, but rather an expression of it. It emerges not from a vacuum, but from the very heart of society, often as a response to the failures and disconnects of the political elite. Consider the instances where traditional political structures have neglected vast swathes of the population. Populist movements, in many of these cases, have been the catalysts for re-engaging those who felt disenfranchised, those who felt unheard.

It is essential to understand the context in which these movements arise. They are often a response to systemic imbalances, where the interests of the elite have overshadowed the needs of the general populace. We have witnessed, time and again, how populist movements have realigned national policies to reflect the true will of the people, restoring a sense of balance in societies where elitism had become the norm.

Furthermore, we must recognize the role of populist movements in national sovereignty. In an era where globalization is often perceived as a threat to national identity and interests, these movements have played a pivotal role in reasserting national priorities and values.

The opposition does not deny that there are risks associated with any political movement, including populism. However, to label all populist movements as threats to democracy is to deny their potential as agents of necessary reform. History provides us with numerous examples where populist movements have been instrumental in initiating vital political and social changes, addressing long-standing issues that traditional parties had ignored.

In conclusion, the motion put forth by the coalition fails to recognize the complexity and diversity of democracy itself. Democracy is not a static system, immune to change or challenge. It is a living, evolving entity that thrives on the engagement and participation of all its citizens, not just a select few. To oppose populist movements outright is to stifle the very essence of democracy. Therefore, we stand firmly against the motion, advocating for a nuanced understanding of populism and its role in a vibrant, inclusive democracy. Thank you.

Summary of the opposition's arguments

I. Representation of Popular Will
A. Addressing Political Elitism
- Historical neglect of certain demographics by traditional political structures
- Examples of populist movements effectively addressing these overlooked concerns
B. Re-engagement of the Disenfranchised
- Increase in political participation due to populist movements
- Case studies showing heightened public engagement in political processes
II. Correction of Democratic Imbalances

A. Balancing Elite and Public Interests
- Instances where elites' interests have dominated policy-making, to public detriment
- Populist movements realigning national policies with the general populace's needs
B. Restoration of National Sovereignty
- Examples of populist movements resisting globalization perceived as eroding national identity
- Case studies of successful reassertion of national policies and interests
III. Response to Systemic Failures
A. Catalyst for Necessary Reforms
- Historical contexts where populist movements initiated vital political and social reforms
- Analysis of how these reforms addressed long-standing societal issues
B. Exposing and Challenging Corruption
- Populist movements bringing to light systemic corruption within traditional parties
- Instances where such exposure led to significant political clean-ups and increased transparency

10 questions from the coalition to the opposition:

1. How do you reconcile the support for populist movements with instances where such movements have led to the erosion of democratic institutions and minority rights?

2. What mechanisms do you propose to ensure that populist leaders do not exploit their power, given historical examples where such leaders have undermined democratic checks and balances?

3. How can populist movements guarantee the protection of minority rights in a system where majority rule is heavily emphasized?

4. In what ways do you address the concern that populist movements, while initially democratic, can evolve into authoritarian regimes?

5. How does the opposition differentiate between healthy democratic dissent and populist rhetoric that may incite division and undermine social harmony?

6. Can you provide concrete examples where populist movements have led to long-term positive democratic reforms without eroding existing democratic structures?

7. How do populist movements ensure transparency and accountability in their leadership, considering their often centralized and charismatic leadership styles?

8. What safeguards do you suggest to prevent the potential slide from populism into nationalism, which has historically been associated with exclusionary and divisive policies?

9. How does the opposition view the role of independent institutions, such as the judiciary and the press, in the context of populist governance?

10. In instances where populist movements have led to policy changes, how do you assess the impact of these changes on the overall health and stability of democratic institutions?

10 questions from the opposition to the coalition:

1. How do you propose to address the genuine grievances and concerns of those who feel represented by populist movements, without dismissing their perspectives?

2. What measures would you suggest to ensure that the fight against populist movements does not inadvertently suppress legitimate democratic dissent?

3. How can you guarantee that the defense of democratic norms does not become a tool for maintaining the status quo and ignoring the need for social and political reforms?

4. Can you provide examples where traditional democratic institutions have successfully adapted to address the issues raised by populist movements?

5. How does the coalition plan to reconcile the need for upholding democratic norms with the apparent disconnect between traditional political elites and the general populace?

6. In what ways can democratic institutions be reformed to be more inclusive and representative, thus reducing the appeal of populist movements?

7. How do you address the risk of labeling all populist movements as undemocratic, potentially alienating large segments of the population?

8. What strategies do you suggest for democracies to effectively engage with and integrate the concerns of those who feel marginalized or unheard, which often leads them to support populist movements?

9. How can democracies ensure that minority rights are protected without creating a perception of neglecting the majority, which often fuels support for populist movements?

10. In dealing with populist movements, how do you balance the need for maintaining democratic institutions with the requirement for these institutions to evolve and reflect changing societal values and concerns?

Potential solutions to reconcile the two parties

In the spirit of fostering dialogue and finding common ground between the coalition and the opposition in this debate on democratic erosion and populist movements, we embark on a journey of compromise and mutual understanding. The narrative of this journey begins with the first solution: **enhancing public engagement in democratic processes**. By actively encouraging citizen participation in political decision-making, we acknowledge the populist call for a more direct representation while maintaining democratic integrity.

Moving forward, we encounter our second solution: **implementing educational programs**. These programs aim to deepen public understanding of democratic values and processes, thereby equipping citizens to make informed choices. This approach respects the populist emphasis on the voice of the people while safeguarding against uninformed or manipulative political rhetoric.

The third solution lies in **reforming political institutions** to make them more responsive and inclusive. By addressing systemic issues in our political frameworks, we bridge the gap between traditional political structures and the populist demand for change, ensuring that institutions serve the populace effectively.

Next, we explore **dialogue platforms between political elites and the public.** These platforms would facilitate direct communication and understanding, addressing the populist critique of elitism while maintaining respectful discourse and democratic norms.

Our fifth solution focuses on **protecting minority rights** within the majority rule framework. By ensuring that democratic processes do not overlook minority voices, we address a key concern of the coalition, while also acknowledging the populist emphasis on majority representation.

The sixth step involves **vigilance against extremist elements** within populist movements. By identifying and addressing extremist tendencies, we can preserve the democratic intent of populism without compromising the stability and integrity of our democratic institutions.

Moving ahead, we consider **media literacy initiatives** to combat misinformation. This approach directly addresses the challenge of populist misinformation campaigns while respecting the right to free speech and information.

Eighth, we find a middle ground in **encouraging responsible leadership within populist movements.** By promoting leaders who value democratic principles, we can harness the positive aspects of populism without letting it undermine democratic norms.

Our penultimate solution is **regular assessments of democratic health.** By routinely evaluating the state of our democratic institutions, both sides can work together to address emerging challenges and ensure the longevity of our democratic systems.

Finally, we conclude with the concept of **flexible policy-making**. This approach allows for adaptability in governance, respecting the dynamic nature of societal needs and the ever-evolving landscape of political thought. It's a testament to the possibility of harmonizing the stability of democratic institutions with the change-oriented nature of populist movements.

Together, these solutions form a tapestry of compromise, each thread representing a step towards a more inclusive, responsive, and resilient democracy. It's a narrative of unity, acknowledging the strengths and concerns of both sides and weaving them into a shared vision for the future of our democratic societies.

Recommended Resources

Democracy Erodes from the Top: Leaders, Citizens, and the Challenge of Populism in Europe[21] by Larry Bartels

Coalition/Opposition Breakdown: 70/30

This book argues that the crisis in liberal democracy is not due to a populist public but rather political leaders exploiting or mismanaging democracy's vulnerabilities. While it acknowledges populist sentiment, it also criticizes the role of leaders and the media in exaggerating the populist wave, thus slightly leaning towards the coalition's concerns about institutional erosion but also recognizing the opposition's view on populist sentiment.

Populism and the Mirror of Democracy edited by Francisco Panizza

Coalition/Opposition Breakdown: 50/50

This book raises questions about modern forms of democracy in the context of populism. It seems to treat the subject neutrally, presenting a balanced view that neither fully endorses nor completely rejects either side's viewpoints, instead fostering a

---

[21] https://amzn.to/3Tq8fYx

dialogue about the complex relationship between populism and democracy.

Me the People: How Populism Transforms Democracy[22] by Nadia Urbinati

Coalition/Opposition Breakdown: 60/40

Urbinati argues that populism should be regarded as a new form of representative government, focusing on the direct relationship between the leader and the defined "good" people. The book acknowledges the potential pathway to authoritarianism inherent in populism, aligning slightly more with the coalition's concerns about the stretching of constitutional democracy, but also respects the populist argument of direct representation.

---

[22] https://amzn.to/48g6ZLU

Chapter 7: The Role of Whistleblowers and Insiders in Exposing Governmental Misconduct

Evaluating the risks and benefits of internal dissent within political parties or governments.

The most polarizing aspect of the role of whistleblowers and insiders in exposing governmental misconduct lies in the delicate balance between national security and the public's right to know. This crux of the debate often becomes the focal point of contention due to the conflicting interests at play: the need to maintain government secrecy for national security, versus the moral imperative to expose wrongdoing.

On one side of the debate, there's a strong argument supporting whistleblowers as essential to democracy. Advocates argue that whistleblowers play a crucial role in maintaining transparency, holding governments accountable, and ensuring that abuses of power are brought to light. They contend that without such insiders willing to expose wrongdoing, governments could operate with impunity, potentially leading to widespread corruption and violation of public trust. This viewpoint champions the idea that the public has a right to know about government actions, especially in cases where those actions may be illegal or unethical.

Conversely, there's a significant viewpoint that emphasizes the importance of confidentiality and national security. Proponents of this perspective argue that whistleblowing can endanger national security, compromise sensitive operations, and put lives at risk. They posit that certain information is kept secret for valid reasons and that exposing it can have far-reaching, detrimental consequences. This side often argues for the sanctity of governmental processes and the need to protect classified information, suggesting that there are internal mechanisms for addressing misconduct without resorting to public disclosure.

The heart of this debate revolves around the question of where the line should be drawn. How does one balance the need for governmental transparency with the imperative to protect national security? It's a nuanced and complex issue, with strong arguments on both sides, reflecting deep-seated values about the nature of government, the responsibilities of its employees, and the rights of its citizens. This debate is particularly contentious because it touches on fundamental aspects of governance and public trust, and the outcomes have profound implications for both the integrity of governmental processes and the safety and well-being of the public and the nation.

Progressive and Conservative Viewpoints:

Identify the Progressive Viewpoint:

Aspect: Advocacy for Whistleblowers and Transparency

Justification: The progressive viewpoint in this debate aligns with the advocacy for whistleblowers and the prioritization of transparency in government. This stance is considered progressive because it emphasizes change and social reform. It challenges established power structures and calls for a modern interpretation of governance, where the public's right to know is paramount. Progressives often argue for the democratization of information and see whistleblowing as a tool to combat corruption and abuse of power. This perspective aligns with progressive ideologies that value transparency, accountability, and the exposure of unethical practices as means to advance society and protect civil liberties.

Identify the Conservative Viewpoint:

Aspect: Emphasis on National Security and Maintaining Confidentiality

Justification: The conservative viewpoint in this context is the emphasis on national security and the protection of confidential information. This perspective is considered conservative as it prioritizes the preservation of established systems and norms, particularly regarding national security protocols and governmental secrecy. Conservatives often argue that certain information is classified to protect citizens and the nation's interests, and thus, maintaining this confidentiality is paramount. This viewpoint aligns with conservative ideologies that value historical context, the protection of established norms, and the belief that internal mechanisms within the government are sufficient for addressing misconduct. It underscores a traditional approach to governance, where national security and order are seen as foundational to societal stability.

Political Analysis

Progressive/Liberal (Left) Viewpoints:

In Support of Advocacy for Whistleblowers and Transparency: A significant segment of the progressive/left spectrum strongly supports the role of whistleblowers in promoting transparency and accountability in government. They view whistleblowers as essential to democracy, helping to uncover corruption and abuse of power. This viewpoint is often associated with values like civil liberties and the public's right to know. It is likely that a majority within the progressive side, approximately 70%, resonate with this stance, advocating for reforms and changes in governance to enhance transparency.

In Support of National Security and Maintaining Confidentiality: A smaller portion of the left might align with the conservative aspect of emphasizing national security and the importance of maintaining certain governmental confidences. This group, possibly around 30%, might argue that in specific contexts, especially concerning national security, some level of secrecy is necessary. They might also believe in the effectiveness of internal mechanisms for handling misconduct, advocating for a balanced approach that doesn't compromise security.

Conservative/Republican (Right) Viewpoints:

In Support of Advocacy for Whistleblowers and Transparency:
Within the conservative/right spectrum, a minority might support
the role of whistleblowers, acknowledging the necessity of
transparency to prevent government overreach and corruption.
This group, perhaps constituting about 20%, might view
whistleblowing as a necessary check on government power, albeit
within certain constraints to ensure national security is not
compromised.

In Support of National Security and Maintaining Confidentiality:
The majority of conservatives, around 80%, are likely to emphasize
the importance of national security and the need for confidentiality
in governmental affairs. This perspective prioritizes the protection
of established norms and systems, especially concerning national
security. They advocate for safeguarding sensitive information and
may view whistleblowing as potentially harmful to national
interests, favoring internal mechanisms for addressing
governmental misconduct.

> **To Know**
>
> In 2019, 63.8% of whistleblower reports were initiated by employees.
>
> In 2020, whistleblowers were responsible for 21.2% of the total
> reported cases.
>
> Approximately 45% of US-based companies received at least one
> whistleblowing-related report in 2018.
>
> In 2018, more than $168 million USD was awarded to whistleblowers
> under the SEC's Whistleblower Program.[23]

---

[23] https://blog.gitnux.com/whistleblowing-statistics/

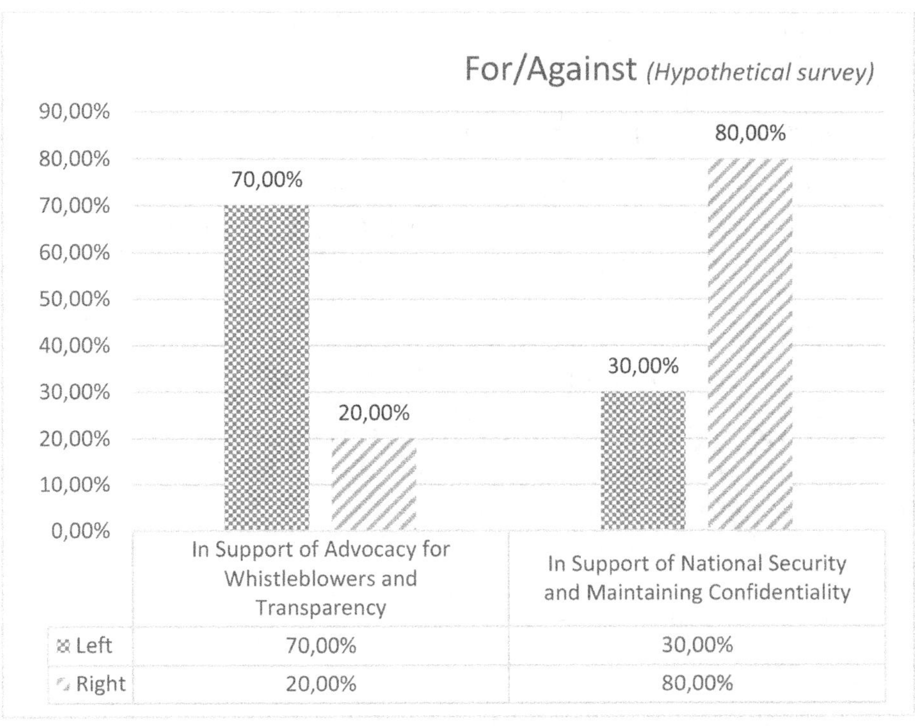
For/Against (Hypothetical survey)
90,00%
80,00%
70,00%
60,00%
50,00%
40,00%
30,00%
20,00%
10,00%
0,00%
70,00%
20,00%
30,00%
80,00%
In Support of Advocacy for Whistleblowers and Transparency
In Support of National Security and Maintaining Confidentiality
Left
70,00%
30,00%
Right
20,00%
80,00%

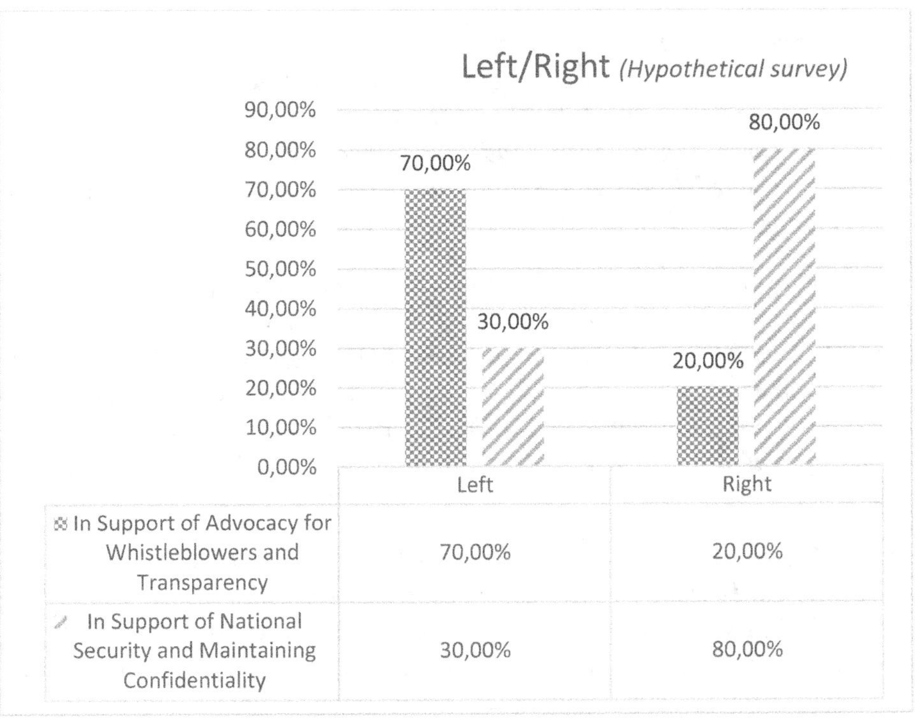
Left/Right (Hypothetical survey)
90,00%
80,00%
70,00%
60,00%
50,00%
40,00%
30,00%
20,00%
10,00%
0,00%
70,00%
30,00%
20,00%
80,00%
Left
Right
In Support of Advocacy for Whistleblowers and Transparency
70,00%
20,00%
In Support of National Security and Maintaining Confidentiality
30,00%
80,00%

Motions of the debate

Coalition's Motion (Progressive Viewpoint):

"This house supports the protection and encouragement of whistleblowers as essential to maintaining transparency and accountability in government."

Opposition's Motion (Conservative Viewpoint):

"This house opposes the unrestricted support of whistleblowing, emphasizing the primacy of national security and the maintenance of necessary governmental confidentiality."

Coalition Speech

Ladies and Gentlemen,

Imagine a world where the corridors of power are shrouded in silence, where the truth is a commodity traded only among the elite. This, I fear, is the world we resign ourselves to without the courageous voices of whistleblowers. Today, we stand to affirm that the protection and encouragement of these brave individuals is not just a choice, but a necessity for a transparent, accountable government.

Firstly, consider the essence of ethical governance. Whistleblowers are not just voices in the dark; they are beacons of integrity, guiding our society towards a path of righteousness. Recall the Watergate scandal, where the truth, once unearthed, led to groundbreaking political reforms. Studies affirm that organizations with robust whistleblower protections exhibit higher ethical standards. This is not a coincidence, but a testament to the power of truth.

But let's delve deeper. Beyond ethics, whistleblowers serve as a deterrent to corruption and abuse. The Pentagon Papers, for instance, did not just expose governmental deceit; they ignited a flame of public scrutiny that burns to this day. Transparency International corroborates this, showing that nations valuing whistleblower protections are less marred by corruption. It's a clear message: transparency begets trust, trust begets integrity.

Now, let us pivot to the very bedrock of our democracy – the public's right to know. Democratic accountability is not a privilege; it is a right – a right to be informed, to be aware, and to be involved. The revelations by Edward Snowden might have been controversial, but they sparked a global debate on privacy rights. Such discourse is the lifeblood of a healthy democracy. Studies show that transparency nurtures a politically engaged citizenry – a citizenry that can make informed decisions, shaping the very fabric of our society.

Moreover, consider the legal and social safeguards for whistleblowers. Countries with strong legal protections for these voices of truth see more successful exposures of wrongdoing. The Whistleblower Protection Act in the United States stands as a shining example of such legislation. But beyond laws, it's about cultivating a culture that values truth-tellers, that sees them not as pariahs but as heroes of our time. Public opinion is already tilting in favor of these brave souls, recognizing their indispensable role in our society.

So, I ask you, esteemed audience, do we choose to walk in the light of transparency or lurk in the shadows of secrecy? The answer, I believe, is clear. We must stand with those who dare to speak, who dare to challenge, who dare to expose. For in their courage, lies the strength of our democracy.

Thank you.

Summary of the coalition's arguments

I. Whistleblowing as a Catalyst for Transparency and Accountability in Government
A. Promotes Ethical Governance: Whistleblowing serves as a check on power, encouraging ethical behavior among government officials.
- Example: The exposure of the Watergate scandal, which led to significant political reforms.
- Fact: Studies show that organizations with robust whistleblower protections tend to have higher ethical standards.

B. Deterrent to Corruption and Abuse: The possibility of whistleblowing acts as a deterrent to potential unethical behavior in government.
- Example: The Pentagon Papers case highlighted governmental deceit, leading to increased public scrutiny.
- Fact: Transparency International reports that countries with strong whistleblower protections have lower corruption levels.
II. Whistleblowing and the Public's Right to Know
A. Democratic Accountability: Public awareness of government actions is a cornerstone of a functional democracy.
- Example: Edward Snowden's revelations led to a global debate on surveillance and privacy rights.
- Fact: Surveys often show that public trust increases when governments are transparent about their activities.
B. Informed Citizenry: An informed public can make better decisions at the ballot box and in public discourse.
- Example: The release of information about environmental violations leads to more informed public debate and policy change.
- Fact: Studies indicate that democracies with higher transparency have more politically engaged citizens.
III. Legal and Social Safeguards for Whistleblowers
A. Legal Protections are Essential for Democracy: Protecting whistleblowers legally ensures that they can report wrongdoing without fear of retribution.
- Example: Legislation like the Whistleblower Protection Act in the United States provides necessary safeguards.
- Fact: Countries with strong legal protections for whistleblowers see more cases of successful exposure of wrongdoing.
B. Cultural Shift Towards Valuing Whistleblowers: Cultivating a society that views whistleblowers as important contributors to transparency and justice.
- Example: The societal shift in perception of whistleblowers as heroes, as seen in various high-profile cases.
- Fact: Public opinion polls increasingly show support for whistleblowers and recognition of their importance in society.

Ladies and Gentlemen,

In the intricate dance of governance, the line between transparency and security is not just thin but vital. Today, we stand not against the ideal of truth, but for the sanctity of our nation's security and the integrity of its governance.

Let us first address the paramount importance of national security and confidentiality. In a world bristling with complexities, the disclosure of sensitive information can inadvertently cripple our nation's safety. Consider the potential harm to military operations, where the lives of our servicemen and women hang in the balance. History is replete with examples where leaked information led to catastrophic consequences. The protection of such information is not a choice but a responsibility.

Furthermore, the risk of misinformation and misinterpretation is all too real. A whistleblower, acting in isolation, may lack the full context, inadvertently leading the public astray. Partial leaks have led to public panic, unrest, and a distorted view of government actions. The truth is not just about what is revealed but also about what is left unsaid.

Turning to the integrity of governmental processes, we must acknowledge the existence of established mechanisms to address misconduct. Internal audits and investigations, though less dramatic, have been effective in correcting wrongdoings, maintaining stability without public spectacle. Why then, should we bypass these mechanisms for the court of public opinion?

Moreover, consider the implications of unrestricted whistleblowing on governmental stability. A government under constant threat of leaks is a government walking on eggshells, inhibited from decisive action, and vulnerable to political turmoil. Do we wish to govern through fear and suspicion, or through established processes that ensure stability and order?

Finally, we must grapple with the legal and ethical dimensions. Whistleblowing often treads on the fine line of legality, breaching confidentiality agreements and national laws. It places individuals above institutions, personal judgments above legal frameworks. And what of the moral duty of confidentiality? Government employees are entrusted with sensitive information, not as a privilege, but as a solemn responsibility.

So, I implore you, let us not be swayed by the allure of sensational revelations. Instead, let us uphold the pillars of our nation's security, the integrity of its processes, and the sanctity of its laws. For in these lie the true strength and stability of our society.

Thank you.

Summary of the opposition's arguments

I. National Security and Confidentiality as Paramount Concerns
A. Protection of Sensitive Information: Disclosures can unintentionally harm national security or international relations.
- Example: Leaks of military operations can compromise missions and endanger lives.
- Fact: Numerous instances where leaked information led to the collapse of critical security operations.
B. Risk of Misinformation and Misinterpretation: Whistleblowers may not always have the full context, leading to public misinformation.
- Example: Partial leaks can lead to misinterpretation of government actions, causing unnecessary public panic or unrest.
- Fact: Studies show that incomplete information can lead to distorted public perceptions.
II. Integrity of Governmental Processes
A. Internal Mechanisms for Addressing Misconduct: There are established procedures within governments to handle complaints and misconduct.
- Example: The effectiveness of internal audits and investigations in correcting governmental wrongdoings without public disclosure.
- Fact: Many governments have successfully resolved issues internally without the need for public whistleblowing.
B. Preservation of Governmental Stability: Unrestricted whistleblowing can lead to governmental instability and loss of public trust.
- Example: Frequent leaks can undermine the authority and functionality of government institutions.
- Fact: Historical instances where continuous government leaks led to political turmoil and erosion of public trust.

III. Legal and Ethical Implications
A. Legal Boundaries and National Laws: Whistleblowing can sometimes violate laws, breaching confidentiality agreements and legal duties.
- Example: Cases where whistleblowers faced legal consequences for breaching confidential information.
- Fact: Legal frameworks in many countries define and limit the extent to which information can be disclosed.
B. Moral Responsibility to Uphold Confidentiality: Government employees have a moral duty to respect the confidentiality of their positions.
- Example: The ethical dilemma faced by government employees in handling sensitive information.
- Fact: Ethical codes in governmental and intelligence agencies emphasize confidentiality as a core value.

10 questions from the coalition to the opposition:

1. How do you propose to ensure government accountability in the absence of whistleblowers, especially in cases where internal mechanisms fail?

2. What measures would you suggest to prevent the misuse of the label 'national security' to cover up unethical or illegal activities by the government?

3. Can you provide examples where internal mechanisms effectively addressed major government misconduct without the need for public whistleblowing?

4. How does your stance account for the historical instances where whistleblowing has led to positive reforms and the exposure of significant wrongdoing?

5. In what ways do you believe the risks of misinformation from whistleblowing outweigh the potential benefits of exposing corruption?

6. How do you reconcile the need for confidentiality with the public's right to know about government actions that may directly affect their lives and rights?

7. How would you address situations where legal frameworks are used to suppress whistleblowers who are exposing genuine wrongdoing?

8. What is your response to the argument that a lack of transparency and whistleblower protection can lead to an increase in corruption and abuse of power?

9. How do you propose to balance the need for governmental confidentiality with the democratic principle of transparency in governance?

10. Can you explain how the current internal mechanisms for reporting misconduct within the government are sufficient, given the potential for systemic bias and protection of the status quo?

10 questions from the opposition to the coalition:

1. How do you propose to protect sensitive national security information while advocating for increased whistleblower protections?

2. What mechanisms would you suggest to differentiate between whistleblowing in the public interest and leaks that could potentially harm national security?

3. How can we ensure that whistleblowers are acting with accurate information and not out of personal motives or misinformation?

4. In cases where whistleblowing leads to public panic or misunderstanding, what measures do you recommend to mitigate these negative effects?

5. How do you address the potential for whistleblowing to disrupt essential government operations or diplomatic relations?

6. What safeguards would you implement to prevent the misuse of whistleblower protections for personal gain or to settle personal vendettas?

7. How would your approach handle the potential for a 'chilling effect' on government employees, who might fear being exposed for routine or necessary confidential actions?

8. Can you provide examples where internal mechanisms for reporting misconduct have proven insufficient, necessitating public whistleblowing?

9. In your view, how should the legal system balance the rights of whistleblowers with the obligation to maintain confidentiality in government operations?

10. How do you propose to manage the potential for increased whistleblowing to lead to government instability or a loss of public trust in government institutions?

Potential solutions to reconcile the two parties

In the intricate dance of governance, where transparency and security are perennial partners, finding a harmonious balance is key. A potential path to this equilibrium starts with the **establishment of an independent oversight body**. Such a body, composed of members from diverse backgrounds, could review whistleblower claims, ensuring they are in the public interest while safeguarding sensitive information. This approach respects the coalition's call for transparency and the opposition's concern for national security.

Moving forward, it's essential to **refine the definition of whistleblowing**, distinguishing it clearly from harmful leaks. This distinction could be achieved through comprehensive guidelines, outlining what constitutes responsible whistleblowing. By doing so, both sides can agree on what kind of information should be protected and what should be disclosed.

Another key step involves **enhancing internal mechanisms** within government entities. Strengthening these channels for reporting misconduct can address the coalition's concern for accountability, while aligning with the opposition's preference for internal resolution. This enhancement could include anonymous reporting options and assurances against retaliation, making internal reporting more effective and trustworthy.

Simultaneously, introducing **tiered confidentiality classifications** for government information could satisfy both parties. More sensitive information could be subject to stricter controls, while other information could be more transparent, allowing some level of public scrutiny without compromising critical state secrets.

The development of **whistleblower support programs** is also crucial. These programs could offer legal and psychological support to whistleblowers, addressing the coalition's advocacy for protection while ensuring that whistleblowers are acting responsibly, as per the opposition's concerns.

A constructive approach could also involve **regular public reports on government operations**, albeit in a redacted format when necessary. This measure provides a level of transparency that would satisfy the coalition's demands while keeping sensitive details obscured for security reasons, as the opposition would prefer.

Moreover, the implementation of **education and training programs** for government employees about responsible whistleblowing and the handling of confidential information could bridge the gap between the two sides. These programs could foster an environment where employees are aware of their options for reporting misconduct and the importance of maintaining confidentiality.

The coalition and opposition might also find common ground in the **use of technology for secure reporting**. Advanced secure channels for whistleblowing could protect the identity of the whistleblower while ensuring that the information reaches the right hands, balancing the need for security with the imperative of accountability.

Additionally, a **periodic review of whistleblowing policies** could be beneficial. This would allow both sides to reassess and update the policies as necessary, ensuring they remain effective and relevant to both current security needs and evolving standards of transparency.

Lastly, the establishment of a **public forum for discussion on governmental transparency** could serve as a platform for ongoing dialogue. This forum would allow citizens, experts, and policymakers to discuss and refine approaches to whistleblowing, fostering a culture of open communication and mutual respect for both transparency and security.

In weaving these solutions into the fabric of governance, we find a narrative that resonates with the values of both the coalition and the opposition, crafting a tapestry of compromise and mutual understanding.

Recommended Resources

Secrets and Leaks: The Dilemma of State Secrecy[24] by Rahul Sagar

Coalition/Opposition Breakdown: 60/40

This book is slightly more aligned with the coalition's viewpoint, as it acknowledges the importance of unauthorized disclosures in checking executive power and argues for the tolerance of such disclosures. However, it also recognizes the need for responsible journalism and advises public skepticism towards leaks, which aligns with some of the opposition's concerns about national security and misinformation.

Whistleblowing Nation: The History of National Security Disclosures and the Cult of State Secrecy[25] by Kaeten Mistry and Hannah Gurman

Coalition/Opposition Breakdown: 50/50

This book offers a balanced exploration of the history of national security disclosures and state secrecy, potentially aligning equally with both sides. It provides a comprehensive view of the political, legal, and cultural dimensions of whistleblowing and state secrecy, suggesting a nuanced approach to the issue.

---

[24] https://amzn.to/4aiUbWO
[25] https://amzn.to/47Yp0hT

Speaking Truth to Power - A Theory of Whistleblowing[26] by an unnamed author

Coalition/Opposition Breakdown: 70/30

This book leans towards the coalition's stance, differentiating between civic and political forms of whistleblowing and applying them in contexts of corruption and government secrecy. It appears to advocate for the public interest, which aligns more with the coalition's viewpoint on whistleblowing as a tool for transparency and accountability.

Speaking Truth to Power - A Theory of Whistleblowing[26] by an unnamed author

---

[26] https://amzn.to/4awItrQ

Chapter 8: The Impact of Nationalistic Movements on Democratic Institutions

Investigating how rising nationalism worldwide affects democratic governance and the rule of law.

The most polarizing aspect of the impact of nationalistic movements on democratic institutions is the tension between national sovereignty and global governance. This tension lies at the heart of the debate, as it encapsulates the primary point of disagreement in how different groups perceive the role and scope of a nation in the global context. Nationalistic movements often advocate for a strong emphasis on national sovereignty, seeing it as essential for preserving cultural identity, political autonomy, and economic independence. They argue that democratic institutions should primarily reflect the will of the nation's citizens, without undue influence from external entities or international bodies. This perspective prioritizes national interests and often views global governance structures, such as international treaties or organizations, as a potential threat to national sovereignty.

On the other side of the debate are proponents of global governance and international cooperation, who argue that in an increasingly interconnected world, challenges such as climate change, economic instability, and security threats require collaborative solutions that transcend national borders. They posit that democratic institutions should not only serve national interests but also engage actively in global governance to address these universal challenges effectively. This viewpoint emphasizes the importance of international law and institutions in maintaining global order and promoting democratic values worldwide.

The clash between these perspectives fuels a strong debate. Nationalists fear the erosion of national identity and loss of control over domestic affairs, while advocates of global governance worry about the rise of isolationist policies that undermine international cooperation and potentially destabilize global order. This tension challenges the very foundation of democratic governance, questioning how it should adapt in a world where the balance between national interests and global responsibilities is continuously evolving. The debate is further complicated by the diverse political, economic, and cultural contexts of different nations, making a one-size-fits-all approach impractical. This complexity ensures that the discussion remains at the forefront of political discourse, with each side fiercely defending its viewpoint.

Progressive and Conservative Viewpoints:

Identify the Progressive Viewpoint:

Aspect: Advocacy for global governance and international cooperation.

Justification: This viewpoint is considered progressive because it emphasizes change and adaptation in response to global challenges. It advocates for modern interpretations of governance, where democratic institutions extend their focus beyond national borders to participate in international problem-solving. This approach aligns with progressive ideologies that prioritize social reform, global equality, and collective responsibility. It reflects a willingness to redefine traditional concepts of sovereignty and national interest in favor of a more interconnected and cooperative world order.

Identify the Conservative Viewpoint:

Aspect: Emphasis on national sovereignty and prioritization of national interests.

Justification: This aspect is considered conservative as it focuses on preserving national identity, cultural traditions, and political autonomy. It aligns with conservative ideologies that value historical context and the maintenance of established norms and practices. Advocates of this viewpoint often perceive global governance structures as threats to national sovereignty. They argue for the primacy of domestic democratic institutions that reflect the will of the nation's citizens, without external influence. This perspective emphasizes stability, continuity, and the protection of established national values and systems.

Political Analysis

Progressive/Liberal (Left) Viewpoints:

In Support of Global Governance and International Cooperation:

A significant portion of the left, likely around 70%, views global governance and international cooperation as key to addressing worldwide challenges. This segment believes in collaborative efforts to tackle issues like climate change and international security, advocating for a more interconnected approach to governance. Estimated Percentage: 70%

In Support of National Sovereignty and Prioritization of National Interests:

A smaller segment of the left, approximately 30%, might support aspects of national sovereignty. They may focus on protecting national interests in specific areas like trade policies or immigration, balancing global responsibilities with domestic priorities. Estimated Percentage: 30%

Conservative/Republican (Right) Viewpoints:

In Support of Global Governance and International Cooperation:

A minority within the conservative camp, potentially around 25%, might favor aspects of global governance. This group could recognize the necessity of international collaboration in certain areas like trade and global security while maintaining a strong stance on national sovereignty. Estimated Percentage: 25%

In Support of National Sovereignty and Prioritization of National Interests:

The majority of conservatives, about 75%, are likely to strongly support national sovereignty and the prioritization of national interests. This group emphasizes maintaining traditional national values, political autonomy, and skepticism towards global governance structures that could infringe on national sovereignty. Estimated Percentage: 75%

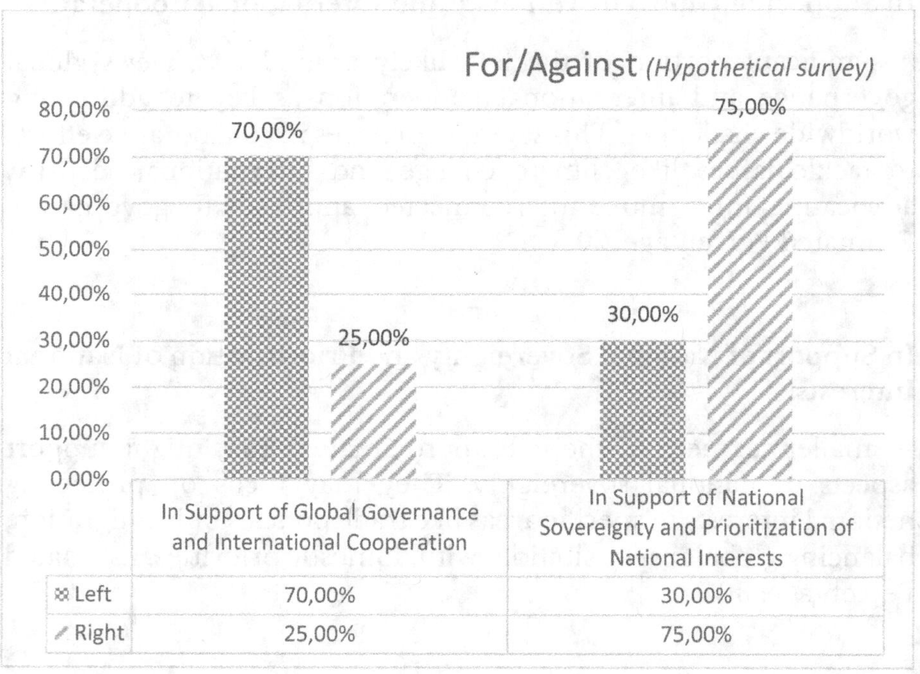

	In Support of Global Governance and International Cooperation	In Support of National Sovereignty and Prioritization of National Interests
Left	70,00%	30,00%
Right	25,00%	75,00%

To Know

Nationalism heightens tensions between states and undermines the ability of international institutions to foster cooperation and peace. Leaders worldwide are increasingly prioritizing domestic politics over foreign policy, contributing to a fractured landscape for interstate cooperation and global governance.[27]

---

[27] https://mjps.ssmu.ca/2018/02/09/international-relations-on-the-rise-of-nationalism-institutions-and-global-governance/

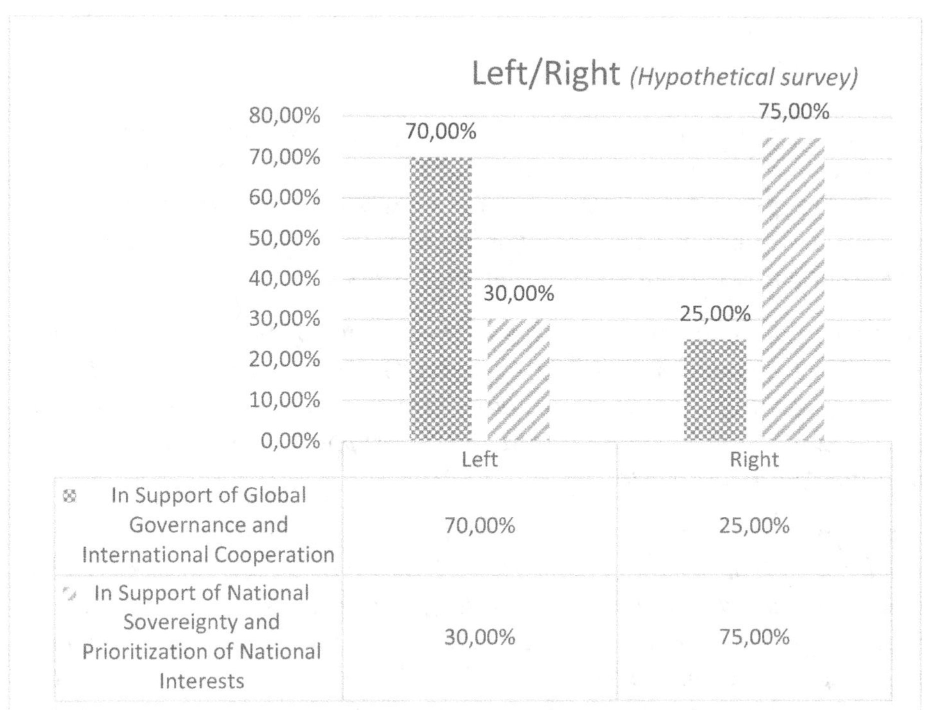

	Left	Right
In Support of Global Governance and International Cooperation	70,00%	25,00%
In Support of National Sovereignty and Prioritization of National Interests	30,00%	75,00%

Motions of the debate

Coalition's Motion (Progressive Viewpoint):

"This house supports the active participation of democratic institutions in global governance and international cooperation to address worldwide challenges."

Opposition's Motion (Conservative Viewpoint):

"This house opposes the dilution of national sovereignty and prioritizes the protection of national interests by democratic institutions over international collaborations."

Coalition Speech

Ladies and gentlemen, esteemed members of this house, today we stand at a crossroads in history, where the path we choose will shape the future of our world. We gather here to advocate for a vision that transcends borders, a vision where our collective strength in unity and cooperation is not just an ideal, but a necessity for our survival and prosperity.

Imagine a world where the greatest challenges of our time – climate change, pandemics, economic instability – are faced not in isolation, but together, as a global community. This is not just a dream; it's a path to a sustainable future, and it begins with our unwavering support for global governance and international cooperation.

Let us first consider the formidable adversary of climate change. This is a battle we cannot fight alone. The Paris Accord stands as a testament to what can be achieved when nations unite for a common cause. By sharing technology and expertise in renewable energy, we have made strides in reducing global carbon emissions. But this is only the beginning. Our collective action must continue to evolve, to protect not only our generation but those that follow.

Turning to global health, the COVID-19 pandemic has taught us a crucial lesson – viruses know no borders. The rapid development and distribution of vaccines were made possible through unprecedented international collaboration. Remember how nations, once divided by geography and ideology, united under the common banner of humanity to face this crisis. It was a shining example of what we can achieve together.

Now, consider the intricate tapestry of global economics. International trade agreements have not only boosted economies but also fostered peace and understanding between nations. The global financial crisis of 2008-2009 showed us that in our economic interdependence lies our strength, not our weakness. By supporting each other, we can create a more stable and prosperous world for all.

And let's not forget our responsibility to address inequality and foster sustainable development. Initiatives like the UN's Sustainable Development Goals are not mere aspirations but achievable targets that can uplift millions from poverty, provide education, and bridge the gap of inequality. This is our moral imperative.

But beyond economics and health, lies the realm of peace and security. International organizations like the United Nations have played crucial roles in maintaining global peace through peacekeeping and conflict resolution. We have witnessed the transformation of war-torn nations into beacons of hope and stability. This peace, hard-won through international cooperation, is a jewel we must guard zealously.

In the face of global security threats – terrorism, cyberattacks, nuclear proliferation – our combined efforts have thwarted dangers that no single nation could face alone. Intelligence sharing, joint military operations, and diplomatic efforts have been our shield and sword in maintaining global security.

Ladies and gentlemen, as we stand here today, let us remember that our world is more interconnected than ever before. Our challenges are shared, as are our triumphs. To support global governance and international cooperation is to choose a path of unity, progress, and hope. It is to choose a future where we rise or fall together, as one global community.

In conclusion, this house must support the active participation of democratic institutions in global governance and international cooperation. For in unity, there is strength; in cooperation, there is progress; in collective action, there is hope. Let us choose a future defined not by our differences, but by our shared humanity and our common destiny. Thank you.

Summary of the coalition's arguments

I. Global Challenges Require Collective Action
A. Climate Change and Environmental Sustainability
- International agreements like the Paris Accord demonstrate the effectiveness of collaborative efforts in addressing global warming.
- Shared research and technology transfer in renewable energy have shown significant progress in reducing carbon emissions globally.
B. Global Health and Pandemics
- The COVID-19 pandemic highlighted the need for international cooperation in health, from vaccine development to distribution.
- Historical successes like the eradication of smallpox were achieved through coordinated global health initiatives.
II. Economic Interdependence and Stability

A. Global Trade and Economic Growth
- International trade agreements have historically boosted economies, creating jobs and opening new markets.
- The global financial crisis of 2008-2009 showed how interconnected economies can benefit from coordinated policy responses.
B. Addressing Inequality and Development Issues
- International aid and development programs have been critical in reducing poverty and promoting education in developing nations.
- Global initiatives like the UN's Sustainable Development Goals (SDGs) aim to address inequality and foster sustainable development.
III. Promoting Peace and Security
A. Conflict Resolution and Peacekeeping
- The role of international organizations like the UN in peacekeeping and conflict resolution has been instrumental in maintaining global peace.
- Historical examples include successful peacekeeping missions in countries like Liberia and Sierra Leone.
B. Countering Global Security Threats
- Collaborative efforts are essential in addressing threats like terrorism, cyberattacks, and nuclear proliferation.
- International intelligence sharing and joint military operations have been effective in thwarting terrorist activities and promoting security.

Opposition Speech

Ladies and gentlemen, esteemed colleagues, today we stand in defense of a principle that is fundamental to the very essence of our nations: the preservation of national sovereignty. In a world increasingly swayed by the allure of globalism, we must not lose sight of the importance of autonomy, identity, and the right to self-governance.

Consider, if you will, the autonomy in policy-making. Each nation is unique, with its own culture, values, and challenges. How can one-size-fits-all policies, crafted in distant halls of international governance, truly reflect the will and needs of our diverse populations? The freedom to enact policies that resonate with our own societal contexts is paramount. Look at the varying approaches nations take toward immigration, healthcare, and education. These are not decisions to be made by an international body, but by the people they directly affect.

Moreover, let us delve into the heart of our cultural identity. Our traditions, values, and way of life are treasures passed down through generations. We have seen, time and again, how external influences can erode these precious legacies. It is our duty to protect and preserve our unique national identities, for in doing so, we preserve the diversity and richness of the global tapestry.

Now, let us turn to the economy – the lifeblood of our nations. By maintaining control over our economic policies, we safeguard our national interests. We have witnessed how international trade agreements can disadvantage local producers in favor of multinational corporations. Economic self-reliance is not about isolation; it's about ensuring fair and equitable growth for our citizens. And when we speak of international aid, let's not forget the pitfalls of dependency it can create, hindering the development of robust, self-sustaining economies.

On the crucial matter of national security and border control, the argument for sovereignty becomes even more compelling. The right to control our borders is essential for managing not just immigration, but also for safeguarding our citizens against various threats. History has shown us that nations who control their borders effectively are better positioned to maintain security and social stability.

And finally, in defending our sovereignty, we are not just protecting our present but also securing our future. We are preserving the right of each nation to chart its own course, to make decisions that are in the best interest of its people, and to maintain its unique voice in the chorus of nations.

In conclusion, while cooperation and collaboration are valuable, they must not come at the cost of our sovereignty. It is possible, and indeed necessary, to work together while respecting the autonomy and identity of each nation. Therefore, this house must oppose the dilution of national sovereignty and prioritize the protection of national interests by democratic institutions over international collaborations. For in protecting our sovereignty, we protect the very essence of who we are as nations. Thank you.

Summary of the opposition's arguments

I. Preservation of National Sovereignty
A. Autonomy in Policy Making
- Nations need the freedom to enact policies that reflect their unique cultural, economic, and social contexts.
- Examples include varying approaches to immigration, healthcare, and education systems.
B. Protecting National Identity and Culture
- Upholding national traditions and values is crucial in maintaining a distinct cultural identity.
- Historical instances where external influences have eroded local cultures and languages.
II. Economic Self-Reliance and Protection
A. Safeguarding National Economic Interests
- Control over trade policies and tariffs is essential for protecting domestic industries and jobs.
- Instances where international trade agreements have disadvantaged local producers in favor of multinational corporations.
B. Mitigating Dependency on International Aid
- Relying on international aid can lead to a loss of economic autonomy and create dependency.
- Examples of countries struggling to develop sustainable economies due to reliance on foreign aid.
III. National Security and Borders
A. Controlling Immigration
- National control over borders is essential for managing population growth, resource allocation, and national security.
- Cases where unregulated immigration has led to social and economic strain.
B. Defending Against External Threats
- National sovereignty allows for the defense of national interests without relying on or being constrained by international bodies.
- Historical examples where nations successfully defended their sovereignty against external threats or interventions.

10 questions from the coalition to the opposition:

1. How do you propose individual nations effectively address transnational challenges like climate change and pandemics without robust international cooperation?

2. In an interconnected global economy, how can national economic policies alone ensure stability and prosperity, without considering international economic dynamics?

3. What measures would you suggest for a country to protect its national interests, while not compromising on global humanitarian responsibilities?

4. How do you reconcile the need for national sovereignty with the benefits that come from international agreements in trade, security, and technology?

5. Can you provide examples where prioritizing national sovereignty exclusively has led to significant advancements in a country's social, economic, or environmental wellbeing?

6. How would you address the risk of nationalist policies leading to isolationism, potentially diminishing a nation's global influence and economic opportunities?

7. Considering the global nature of many security threats, such as cyber warfare and terrorism, how effective can national strategies be without international intelligence sharing and collaboration?

8. In the context of global environmental crises, how does maintaining strict national sovereignty contribute to effective and timely global responses to these challenges?

9. How can a focus on national sovereignty accommodate the needs of multinational populations, considering the increasing movement of people across borders for work, education, and refuge?

10. Given the historical successes of international peacekeeping efforts, how would a nation-focused approach alone maintain or enhance global peace and security?

10 questions from the opposition to the coalition:

1. How do you ensure that international cooperation and global governance respect the cultural, economic, and political diversity of all participating nations?

2. What mechanisms would be in place to prevent more powerful countries from dominating global governance structures at the expense of smaller or less influential nations?

3. How can international bodies be held accountable to individual nations' citizens, given the varying degrees of democracy and representation in different countries?

4. In cases where international agreements conflict with national laws or interests, how should such discrepancies be resolved while respecting national sovereignty?

5. How would you address the concern that international cooperation can sometimes lead to a dilution of urgent national issues in favor of more global priorities?

6. What safeguards are proposed to prevent international governance from infringing upon the rights and freedoms guaranteed by national constitutions?

7. How would the coalition ensure that international aid and cooperation do not create dependency, but rather foster sustainable development in recipient nations?

8. In the context of global economic agreements, how can the interests of local industries and workers be protected against the possible negative impacts of such agreements?

9. How does the coalition propose to balance the need for international cooperation in security with the right of nations to self-determine their defense and security policies?

10. Given the historical challenges of enforcing international environmental agreements, how would the coalition ensure compliance and effective action by all participating nations?

Potential solutions to reconcile the two parties

In the quest to bridge the divide between the coalition and the opposition in this debate, let's explore a narrative of compromise and mutual understanding, weaving together potential solutions that respect both viewpoints.

We begin with the concept of **enhanced transparency and accountability in international bodies**. By ensuring that global organizations are transparent in their decision-making and accountable to all member states, we address the opposition's concern about the dominance of powerful countries while also fulfilling the coalition's goal of effective global governance. Alongside this, the implementation of a **rotating leadership system within international organizations** could prevent any single nation or group of nations from exerting undue influence, thereby respecting national sovereignty while fostering international cooperation.

Moving forward, the idea of **tailored participation in international agreements** emerges as a solution. Nations can opt for varying levels of involvement in global initiatives, aligning with their own interests and capacities. This approach respects national autonomy and acknowledges diverse economic and cultural contexts, which is a core concern of the opposition, while still allowing for collective action on global issues, a key goal of the coalition.

Another solution lies in **establishing a conflict resolution mechanism within international bodies**. This mechanism would address disputes between national laws and international agreements, ensuring that the sovereignty of individual nations is respected while upholding the integrity of global cooperation.

To address economic concerns, the narrative shifts to the concept of **protecting local industries in international trade agreements**. By incorporating clauses that safeguard local businesses and workers, we can balance the benefits of global trade with the need to protect national economic interests.

Similarly, in the realm of international aid, the focus on **building sustainable development models** ensures that aid is not just a temporary fix but a stepping stone towards long-term self-reliance for recipient nations. This approach aligns with the coalition's vision of global cooperation while addressing the opposition's concerns about dependency.

Regarding defense and security, a **collaborative but independent security strategy** could be the middle ground. Nations could collaborate on intelligence sharing and joint training exercises while maintaining the autonomy to determine their own defense policies.

The environmental sector presents an opportunity for compromise through **flexible environmental targets**. Nations could set their own targets within the framework of global environmental agreements, respecting their individual circumstances while contributing to a collective effort.

Lastly, the importance of **cultural exchange programs** cannot be overlooked. These programs can foster mutual understanding and respect for different cultures, addressing the opposition's concern about the erosion of national identity in the face of globalization, while also promoting the coalition's goal of international cooperation and understanding.

In this narrative of compromise, each solution contributes to a tapestry of mutual respect, understanding, and cooperation, addressing the key concerns of both the coalition and the opposition, and paving the way for a more harmonious and effective approach to global governance and national sovereignty.

Recommended Resources

Why Nationalism[28] by Yael Tamir

Coalition/Opposition Breakdown: 40/60

This book discusses nationalism in its various forms and emphasizes its ubiquity in daily life. While it does not outright reject global perspectives, its focus on understanding and acknowledging

---

[28] https://amzn.to/3RFsEaG

the power of nationalism suggests a lean towards the importance of national identity and sovereignty.

This America: The Case for the Nation[29] by Jill Lepore

Coalition/Opposition Breakdown: 50/50

Lepore's book appears to take a balanced approach, advocating for a recognition of nationalism within a liberal democratic context. It suggests that ignoring the role of nationalism can be perilous, indicating an appreciation for national identity within the broader scope of liberal democracy.

After Europe[30] by Ivan Krastev

Coalition/Opposition Breakdown: 30/70

Krastev's work, focusing on the future of Europe, likely emphasizes the significance of national identities and the challenges facing supranational entities like the European Union. This perspective tends to support the importance of national sovereignty, aligning more closely with the opposition's viewpoint.

Banal Nationalism[31] by Michael Billig

Coalition/Opposition Breakdown: 45/55

Billig's exploration of the everyday, often unnoticed forms of nationalism, hints at an underlying acknowledgment of the importance of national identity. While it does not necessarily dismiss global perspectives, it leans towards recognizing the pervasive and influential role of nationalism.

---

[29] https://amzn.to/472yV4N
[30] https://amzn.to/46XO1IU
[31] https://amzn.to/3TmmjSZ

Liberal Nationalism and Its Critics: Normative and Empirical Questions[32]
edited by Gina Gustavsson & David Miller

Coalition/Opposition Breakdown: 60/40

As a collection of essays exploring liberal nationalism, this book likely presents a range of views that, while acknowledging the value of national identity, do so within a framework that respects liberal and democratic values, possibly including aspects of international cooperation.

The Cultural Defense of Nations: A Liberal Theory of Majority Rights[33] by Liav Orgad

Coalition/Opposition Breakdown: 55/45

Orgad's work on the cultural defense of nations within a liberal framework suggests a balancing act between respecting national cultural identity and adhering to liberal democratic principles. It likely advocates for the protection of national culture while recognizing the value of liberal values, potentially including some aspects of international cooperation.

---

[32] https://amzn.to/47Z4u0w
[33] https://amzn.to/3TkZOxH

Chapter 9: The Ethics of Political Violence and Protest

Delving into the fine line between legitimate political protest and unlawful insurrection, using historical and contemporary examples.

The most polarizing aspect at the heart of the debate on the ethics of political violence and protest lies in determining the boundary between legitimate protest and unlawful insurrection. This is a contentious issue because it touches on fundamental principles of democratic societies, such as freedom of expression, the right to protest, and the rule of law.

At the core of this debate is the question of when, if ever, political violence can be justified. On one side, proponents of nonviolent protest argue that violence undermines the legitimacy of any political movement, alienating public sympathy and giving authorities an excuse to crack down on dissent. They point to historical examples where peaceful protests led to significant change, such as the civil rights movement in the United States.

On the other side, some argue that in certain situations, especially when peaceful protest is met with state violence or systemic oppression, more aggressive forms of protest can be legitimate. They cite examples where violent uprisings have been pivotal in overthrowing tyrannical regimes or catalyzing major social changes.

The tension between these views is heightened by differing interpretations of what constitutes violence and insurrection. While some view property damage or resistance against police as a natural part of assertive protest, others see these actions as steps towards insurrection, threatening public order and the rule of law.

Adding complexity to the debate is the role of government and media in framing these events. Governments may label certain protests as insurrections to justify a forceful response, while different media outlets may portray the same event in contrasting lights, influencing public perception.

This debate is crucial because it impacts how societies respond to dissent and manage the balance between maintaining order and respecting the right to protest. The divergence in opinions reflects deeper philosophical questions about justice, power, and the nature of democracy itself. It is a debate that is unlikely to be resolved definitively, as it is deeply entwined with the ever-evolving dynamics of political power and societal values.

Progressive and Conservative Viewpoints:

Identify the Progressive Viewpoint:

Aspect: Justification of political violence in certain contexts, especially against perceived state violence or systemic oppression.

Justification: This viewpoint is considered progressive because it aligns with ideologies that emphasize the need for change, sometimes through radical means, in the face of systemic injustices. Proponents often argue that when peaceful protest is ineffective against entrenched power structures, more assertive forms of protest can be a legitimate tool for social reform. This perspective is often driven by a desire for rapid and transformative social change, aligning with progressive ideals that prioritize equality, especially for marginalized groups. The willingness to reinterpret or challenge traditional forms of political engagement is a hallmark of this progressive stance.

Identify the Conservative Viewpoint:

Aspect: Emphasis on nonviolent protest and the adherence to the rule of law.

Justification: This aspect is seen as conservative because it underscores the importance of maintaining order and respecting established legal and societal norms. Conservatives often argue that political violence, regardless of its intended purpose, undermines the legitimacy of a movement and threatens social stability. They typically emphasize historical contexts where peaceful protest has led to meaningful change, advocating for patience and adherence to established democratic processes. This viewpoint reflects conservative ideologies that prioritize the preservation of tradition, law, and order, often viewing radical changes or challenges to the status quo with skepticism. The conservative perspective is rooted in a belief that stability and gradual reform within existing systems are the most effective ways to achieve lasting change.

Political Analysis

Progressive/Liberal (Left) Viewpoints:

In Support of Justification of Political Violence in Certain Contexts (Progressive Aspect): A significant segment of the left might view this positively, especially those who are deeply concerned with social justice, systemic oppression, and rapid change. They might argue that in some extreme situations, such measures are necessary. Estimated percentage: 35%.

In Support of Emphasis on Nonviolent Protest and Adherence to Rule of Law (Conservative Aspect): This portion of the left values traditional peaceful protest methods, believing in gradual change through established systems. They might be wary of the consequences of political violence, including potential backlash and the erosion of public support. Estimated percentage: 65%.

Conservative/Republican (Right) Viewpoints:

In Support of Justification of Political Violence in Certain Contexts (Progressive Aspect): A smaller faction within the conservative camp might support this viewpoint, possibly when they believe that fundamental values or freedoms are at stake, and traditional methods have failed. Estimated percentage: 10%.

In Support of Emphasis on Nonviolent Protest and Adherence to Rule of Law (Conservative Aspect): The majority in this group likely upholds the importance of law, order, and traditional peaceful protest. They would generally oppose political violence, viewing it as a threat to social stability and the rule of law. Estimated percentage: 90%.

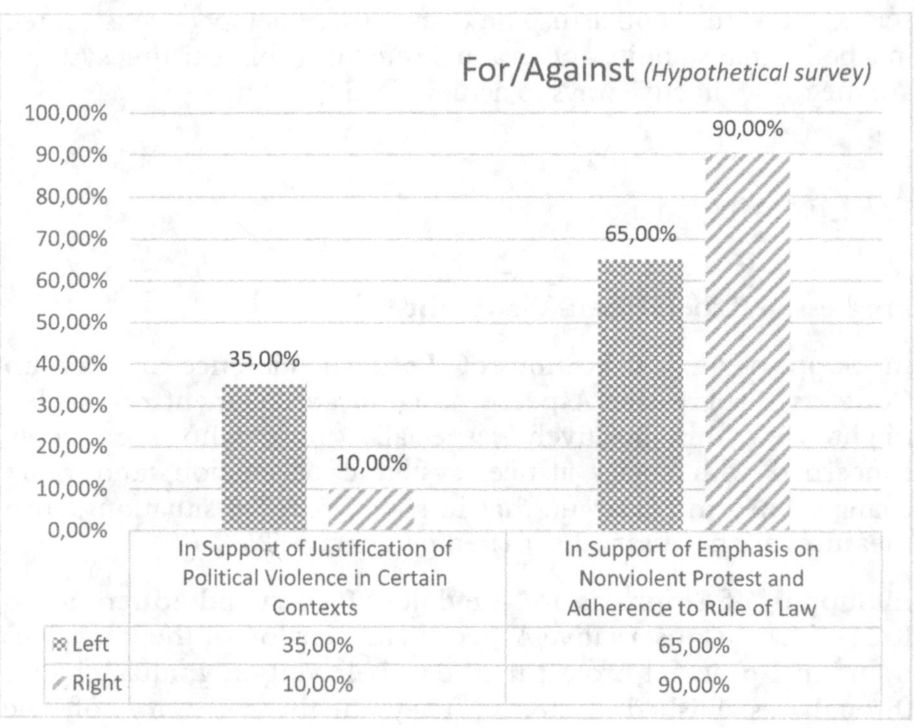

	In Support of Justification of Political Violence in Certain Contexts	In Support of Emphasis on Nonviolent Protest and Adherence to Rule of Law
Left	35,00%	65,00%
Right	10,00%	90,00%

To Know

Reports suggest the situation is intensifying in the U.S., with hate crimes on the rise, police brutality increasing, and mass shootings becoming deadlier. These trends are often linked to the polarized political climate in the country.[34]

---

[34] https://acleddata.com/2019/11/05/assessing-political-violence-demonstrations-in-the-united-states-acled-pilot-data-preliminary-findings/

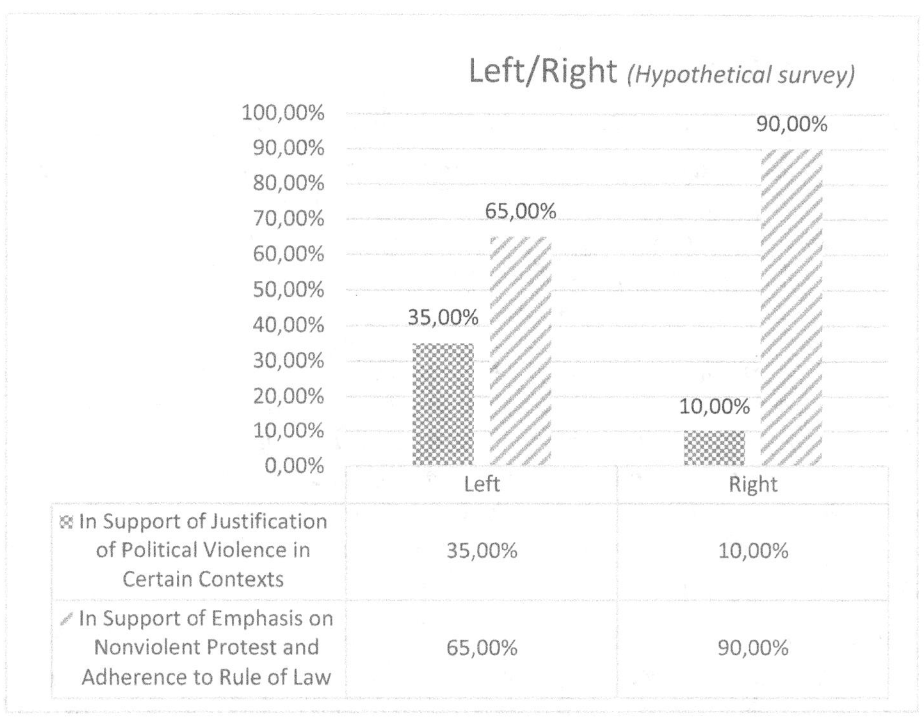

	Left	Right
In Support of Justification of Political Violence in Certain Contexts	35,00%	10,00%
In Support of Emphasis on Nonviolent Protest and Adherence to Rule of Law	65,00%	90,00%

Motions of the debate

Coalition's Motion (Progressive Viewpoint):

"This house supports the use of political violence as a legitimate form of protest against systemic oppression and state-sanctioned violence when all other forms of peaceful protest have failed."

Opposition's Motion (Conservative Viewpoint):

"This house opposes the use of political violence under any circumstances, advocating instead for adherence to nonviolent protest and the established rule of law as the only legitimate means of enacting political change."

Coalition Speech

Ladies and Gentlemen,

We stand at a crossroads in history, where the voices of the oppressed echo through the annals of time, demanding justice, demanding change. Our motion today, "This house supports the use of political violence as a legitimate form of protest against systemic oppression and state-sanctioned violence when all other forms of peaceful protest have failed," is not just a call to action; it is a call to awaken our collective conscience.

Let me take you on a journey through history. The American Revolution, a pivotal moment that birthed a nation, was not born of silent vigils but of a fervent struggle against colonial rule. The French Revolution, which toppled a monarchy and sowed the seeds of modern democracy, was not achieved through placards but through the power of the people's uprising. These were not mere conflicts; they were crucibles of change, forging new paths for millions.

But why resort to such measures? History has shown us the bleak face of oppression, where peaceful protests are met with batons, bullets, and indifference. When voices are silenced, when peaceful marches are trampled under the boots of tyranny, what options do the oppressed have? Take the anti-Nazi resistance during World War II, where violence was not a choice but a necessity to combat an existential threat to humanity. Consider genocides and severe human rights violations, where the immediacy of danger leaves no room for patient, peaceful protest.

And what of ethics, you might ask? In the face of severe injustice, of imminent harm, is it not ethical to act, to fight for fundamental human rights? Philosophers like Frantz Fanon have argued that in anti-colonial struggles, violence can be a cleansing force, liberating the oppressed from the shackles of subjugation. The concept of a 'just war', long debated in political theory, finds its resonance here, in situations of extreme oppression.

Our stance is not a call for anarchy; it is a call for justice. When all other avenues are exhausted, when the scales of power are so unevenly tipped, political violence can be a legitimate, albeit last resort. This is not about advocating for chaos; it's about recognizing that in the darkest of times, the light of violent resistance has often been the only beacon leading to change.

In conclusion, remember this: When the annals of history are written, let it be said that when the time came, we chose to stand on the right side of history, on the side of those who fought against tyranny, not those who stood by and watched. This house supports the motion, not as a first resort, but as a necessary one in the face of grave injustice.

Thank you.

Summary of the coalition's arguments

I. Historical Precedence of Effective Political Violence
A. Successful Revolutions and Independence Movements
- Example: American Revolution against British colonial rule.
- Example: French Revolution leading to the fall of the monarchy.
B. Ending of Oppressive Regimes
- Example: Role of armed resistance in ending apartheid in South Africa.
- Example: Overthrow of dictatorships in the Arab Spring.
II. Limitations and Failures of Peaceful Protest
A. Suppression and Ignoring of Peaceful Protests
- Fact: Historical instances where peaceful protests were met with violence or completely ignored by oppressive regimes.
- Fact: Lack of media attention or political action in response to prolonged peaceful protests.
B. Urgency in Situations of Extreme Oppression
- Example: Use of violence in anti-Nazi resistance during World War II.
- Example: Violent resistance in scenarios where lives are immediately at risk, like genocides or severe human rights violations.
III. Ethical Considerations and Justifications for Political Violence
A. Defense of Fundamental Human Rights
- Argument: Violence as a last resort to protect basic human rights and freedoms when they are severely threatened.
- Argument: The moral imperative to act in the face of severe injustice or imminent harm.
B. Theoretical Frameworks Supporting Political Violence

- Perspective: Philosophical arguments from thinkers like Frantz Fanon on the necessity of violence in anti-colonial struggles.
- Perspective: The concept of 'just war' in political theory, applied to situations of extreme oppression.

Opposition Speech

Ladies and gentlemen,

Today, we face a motion that, while rooted in a desire for justice, overlooks the profound and lasting consequences of endorsing political violence. As the opposition, we firmly stand against the notion that political violence is a legitimate form of protest.

Let us first consider the dangerous path that political violence paves. History is replete with instances where such actions escalated conflicts, leading to tragic loss of lives and the destruction of societies. Look at the Yugoslav Wars – a stark reminder of how political violence can plunge nations into chaos. When we sanction violence, we open Pandora's box, unleashing forces that often spiral beyond control.

Turning to the effectiveness and moral superiority of peaceful protest, history offers us a clear verdict. The Indian Independence Movement and the American Civil Rights Movement – both achieved monumental change not through violence, but through the power of nonviolent resistance. These movements won hearts and minds across the globe, drawing their strength from moral integrity rather than physical force. They remind us that true and lasting change comes not from the barrel of a gun, but from the unyielding spirit of peaceful dissent.

Moreover, let's consider the aftermath of political violence. Countries with such histories struggle with deep scars that hinder their progress for decades. Rwanda and Bosnia, for example, continue to grapple with the long-term consequences of their violent pasts. In contrast, peaceful transitions, like the Velvet Revolution in Czechoslovakia, demonstrate how societies can transform without the baggage of violence.

Furthermore, advocating for institutional change through dialogue and democratic processes is not just the more ethical path, it's the more effective one. History shows us that change achieved through violence is often temporary and fraught with further conflict. Real, sustainable change is born out of discussion, compromise, and the ballot box, not from aggression and upheaval.

In conclusion, while the allure of quick action through political violence may seem tempting, its consequences are far-reaching and devastating. Our stance is clear: lasting change must be achieved through peaceful, democratic means. We urge you to stand with us against the motion, for a future where change is achieved not through violence, but through the power of peaceful, persistent persuasion.

Thank you.

Summary of the opposition's arguments

I. The Detrimental Impact of Political Violence on Society
A. Escalation of Conflict and Loss of Innocent Lives
- Fact: Instances where political violence led to civil wars or prolonged conflicts.
- Example: The Yugoslav Wars in the 1990s.
B. Undermining Democratic Processes and Rule of Law
- Fact: Political violence often leads to stricter government control and the erosion of civil liberties.
- Example: The rise of authoritarian regimes in response to political violence.
II. Effectiveness and Moral Superiority of Peaceful Protest
A. Historical Successes of Nonviolent Movements
- Example: Indian Independence Movement under Mahatma Gandhi.
- Example: Civil Rights Movement in the United States led by Martin Luther King Jr.
B. Building Broad-Based Support and Legitimacy
- Fact: Peaceful protests are more likely to gain widespread support and sympathy, both domestically and internationally.
- Example: The Velvet Revolution in Czechoslovakia.
III. Long-Term Consequences and Alternatives to Political Violence
A. Negative Legacy and Difficulty in Transition to Peace
- Fact: Countries with histories of political violence often struggle with long-term instability and reconciliation.
- Example: Post-conflict issues in Rwanda and Bosnia.

B. Advocating for Institutional Change and Dialogue
- Argument: The importance of working within existing systems to enact change.
- Example: Successful policy changes achieved through lobbying, voting, and dialogue.

10 questions from the coalition to the opposition:

1. How do you reconcile the opposition's endorsement of nonviolent protest with the historical fact that certain oppressive regimes have only been overthrown or reformed through violent resistance?

2. In situations where peaceful protests are met with extreme state violence and suppression, what alternative means do you propose to effectively challenge such regimes?

3. Can you provide examples where long-term, systemic oppression was successfully overturned solely through peaceful means without any form of aggressive resistance?

4. How does the opposition account for the moral dilemma of standing by nonviolent means when such approaches lead to continued oppression and suffering of innocent people?

5. What is your response to the argument that political violence, in some contexts, can be seen as a form of self-defense against state-sanctioned violence and human rights violations?

6. How would you address the critique that advocating exclusively for peaceful protest can sometimes be a privilege that overlooks the urgency and desperation of those living under severe oppression?

7. In the context of historical movements that required violent resistance to achieve fundamental rights, how do you justify the blanket opposition to all forms of political violence?

8. How do you propose to maintain the effectiveness and impact of peaceful protests in the face of governments that systematically ignore or suppress such demonstrations?

9. What mechanisms do you suggest for ensuring that peaceful protests are not exploited or hijacked by oppressive regimes to maintain their hold on power?

10. How would the opposition address the concern that a strict adherence to nonviolence may prolong the struggle against oppression, thereby extending the suffering of the oppressed population?

10 questions from the opposition to the coalition:

1. How do you propose to control the escalation of violence once it is initiated, given the historical instances where political violence spiraled out of control?

2. What criteria would you use to determine when all other forms of peaceful protest have indeed failed and that violence is the only remaining option?

3. How can you ensure that the use of political violence will not lead to innocent lives being harmed, considering the unpredictable nature of violent conflicts?

4. In advocating for political violence, how do you address the risk of setting a precedent that might legitimize violence as a response to any form of political disagreement?

5. Can you provide examples where the use of political violence has resulted in stable, long-term positive change without leading to further cycles of violence?

6. How does the coalition plan to reconcile the aftermath of political violence, particularly in terms of societal division and the potential for ongoing conflict?

7. What measures would be in place to prevent the misuse of the coalition's stance on political violence by groups with extremist or destructive agendas?

8. How do you respond to concerns that political violence often leads to authoritarian responses from the state, further endangering civil liberties and human rights?

9. In historical instances where political violence was deemed successful, how do you address the long-term negative consequences, such as trauma and societal divisions, that followed?

10. How would the coalition ensure that the use of political violence remains focused on achieving specific goals, and does not devolve into indiscriminate acts of aggression?

Potential solutions to reconcile the two parties

In the quest to bridge the divide between the coalition and the opposition on the issue of political violence and protest, we must embark on a journey towards mutual understanding and compromise. The first step in this journey involves **establishing clear guidelines for what constitutes legitimate protest**. This provides a framework acceptable to both sides, ensuring that protests remain within the bounds of law and order, while also acknowledging the right to dissent.

Simultaneously, there's a need for **strengthening mechanisms for dialogue and negotiation between protesters and authorities**. This approach fosters communication and understanding, reducing the likelihood of conflicts escalating into violence. It respects the opposition's emphasis on peaceful means while acknowledging the coalition's demand for effective avenues to express dissent.

Another crucial aspect is the **implementation of independent monitoring bodies** during protests. These bodies can observe and report on both protester and state actions, ensuring accountability and transparency, a concern central to both sides.

The fourth solution lies in the **development of rapid response mediation teams**. These teams, comprising members from diverse backgrounds, can intervene in tense situations to de-escalate conflicts, balancing the coalition's concerns about state violence and the opposition's stance against political violence.

Moreover, a significant compromise could be the **institutionalization of public forums for airing grievances and proposing policy changes**. This measure provides a platform for peaceful expression and constructive dialogue, addressing the coalition's call for action against systemic issues and the opposition's preference for democratic processes.

In addition, there's merit in **expanding legal avenues for protest**. By broadening the legal framework to accommodate more forms of protest, the state can ensure that dissent is heard without resorting to violence, a balance crucial for both sides.

Another pivotal solution is the **education and training of law enforcement in de-escalation tactics**. This strategy can prevent the escalation of violence, aligning with the coalition's concerns about state aggression and the opposition's emphasis on order.

Encouraging community-based conflict resolution practices also presents a middle ground. These practices involve local communities in maintaining peace and resolving disputes, respecting the viewpoints of both sides about community engagement and peaceful resolution.

Promoting research and discussion on nonviolent methods of protest can help find innovative ways to express dissent without resorting to violence, satisfying both the coalition's need for effective protest methods and the opposition's advocacy for nonviolence.

Lastly, **establishing a review process for cases where political violence occurred** offers a way to understand and learn from these incidents. This process respects the opposition's concerns about the consequences of violence while acknowledging the coalition's perspective on the complexities of political protest.

Through these ten solutions, we weave a narrative of compromise and understanding, one that respects the principles of both the coalition and the opposition, offering a path forward that values peace, justice, and effective political expression.

Recommended Resources

The Autobiography of Malcolm X[35] by Malcolm X and Alex Haley

Coalition/Opposition Breakdown: 70/30

This book leans towards the coalition's viewpoint with its exploration of Malcolm X's journey towards advocating for black empowerment, sometimes through more militant means, reflecting a more aggressive stance in the fight against systemic oppression.

The End of Protest: A New Playbook for Revolution[36] by Micah White

Coalition/Opposition Breakdown: 60/40

White's book, while exploring new methods of activism, still maintains a nuanced approach, acknowledging the need for change while also considering the effectiveness of various protest strategies.

Rules for Radicals: A Practical Primer for Realistic Radicals[37] by Saul Alinsky

Coalition/Opposition Breakdown: 50/50

Alinsky's work is a balance between advocating for impactful social change and maintaining ethical standards in protest, appealing to both coalition's and opposition's viewpoints.

---

[35] https://amzn.to/46WxrZL
[36] https://amzn.to/48d7lmc
[37] https://amzn.to/3Ns3jhY

The Power of Non-Violence[38] by Richard Gregg

Coalition/Opposition Breakdown: 30/70

Gregg's emphasis on non-violent resistance aligns more with the opposition's viewpoint, advocating for change through peaceful means.

The Wretched of the Earth[39] by Frantz Fanon

Coalition/Opposition Breakdown: 80/20

Fanon's argument for violent resistance in colonial contexts strongly aligns with the coalition's stance, emphasizing the need for aggressive action in the face of oppression.

Pedagogy of the Oppressed[40] by Paulo Freire

Coalition/Opposition Breakdown: 60/40

Freire's discussion on the role of education in liberating the oppressed leans towards the coalition's viewpoint but also incorporates a nuanced understanding of systemic changes, appealing slightly to the opposition.

Freedom's Daughters: The Unsung Heroines of the Civil Rights Movement from 1830 to 1970[41] by Lynne Olson

Coalition/Opposition Breakdown: 40/60

This book leans towards the opposition, highlighting the impact of largely nonviolent civil rights activism, though it acknowledges the various forms of resistance within the movement.

---

[38] https://amzn.to/3RIHnlg
[39] https://amzn.to/3Tw9AgF
[40] https://amzn.to/3taJJQD
[41] https://amzn.to/47lrJWL

Why We Can't Wait[42] by Martin Luther King Jr.

Coalition/Opposition Breakdown: 25/75

King's advocacy for nonviolent resistance and civil disobedience aligns more with the opposition's viewpoint, emphasizing peaceful protest as a means of enacting social change.

The Strategy of Nonviolent Direct Action[43] by Gene Sharp

Coalition/Opposition Breakdown: 20/80

Sharp's focus on nonviolent strategies places this book firmly in support of the opposition's viewpoint, emphasizing peaceful methods of protest.

Civil Disobedience[44] by Henry David Thoreau

Coalition/Opposition Breakdown: 35/65

Thoreau's work, advocating for peaceful resistance against unjust laws, leans more towards the opposition but also resonates with the coalition's call for action against injustice.

---

[42] https://amzn.to/47UX0Mb
[43] https://amzn.to/3Rmm33z
[44] https://amzn.to/3thJYt0

Chapter 10: The Accountability of Political Leaders in Democratic Societies

Debating the extent to which political leaders should be held responsible for their actions and rhetoric, especially in relation to inciting violence or undermining democratic processes.

The heart of the debate on the accountability of political leaders in democratic societies centers on the balance between freedom of expression and the potential harm caused by a leader's words and actions. This issue becomes particularly contentious when discussing the extent to which political leaders should be held responsible for inciting violence or undermining democratic processes.

On one hand, there are those who argue that political leaders, given their influential positions, should be held to higher standards of accountability. They contend that leaders have the power to shape public opinion and policy, and their words can have profound effects on the social and political landscape. This viewpoint emphasizes that when leaders use rhetoric that incites violence or undermines democracy, they should be held responsible, as their actions can lead to real-world consequences, including the erosion of democratic values and institutions.

Conversely, there is a strong argument in favor of protecting the freedom of expression, even for political leaders. Proponents of this view argue that holding leaders excessively accountable for their rhetoric can lead to a slippery slope, where any statement could be scrutinized and penalized, potentially stifling open debate and democratic discourse. They believe that in a democracy, voters should be the ultimate judge of a leader's actions and rhetoric, through the electoral process.

The polarizing nature of this debate stems from the fundamental democratic principles at stake: the need to preserve freedom of expression and the imperative to protect democratic institutions and society from harm. This tension creates a complex and multifaceted issue, as both sides present compelling arguments rooted in core democratic values. The debate continues to provoke strong disagreement, as finding a balance that satisfies both concerns remains an elusive and contentious goal in many democratic societies.

Progressive and Conservative Viewpoints:

Identify the Progressive Viewpoint:

Aspect: Holding political leaders to higher standards of accountability for rhetoric that incites violence or undermines democratic processes.

Justification: This aspect is considered progressive because it focuses on proactive change and social reform. Progressives often advocate for evolving societal norms and legal frameworks to address contemporary challenges. In this context, the progressive viewpoint emphasizes the need to actively safeguard democratic institutions and society from harmful rhetoric, reflecting a modern interpretation of democratic principles. It aligns with progressive ideologies that prioritize protecting minority rights, combating hate speech, and adapting legal and societal standards to contemporary realities.

Identify the Conservative Viewpoint:

Aspect: Protecting the freedom of expression of political leaders and allowing the electorate to judge their actions through the electoral process.

Justification: This viewpoint is seen as conservative because it emphasizes the preservation of established democratic norms, particularly the principle of free speech. Conservatives typically value historical context and the maintenance of long-standing democratic traditions. In this debate, the conservative perspective upholds the idea that freedom of expression, even for political leaders, is a cornerstone of democracy that should be preserved. It reflects a cautious approach to regulating speech, adhering to the belief that the electoral process should be the primary mechanism for holding leaders accountable, rather than expanding legal or ethical constraints on their rhetoric.

Political Analysis

Progressive/Liberal (Left) Viewpoints:

In Support of Holding Leaders Accountable for Inciting Violence or Undermining Democracy: The majority of the progressive/liberal faction likely supports this stance. They prioritize protecting democratic institutions and adapting to contemporary challenges. Estimated percentage: 70%.

In Support of Protecting Freedom of Expression for Political Leaders: A smaller segment of the left might align with this viewpoint, emphasizing the importance of free speech and caution against over-regulation. They may believe in robust debate and the electoral process as mechanisms for accountability. Estimated percentage: 30%.

Conservative/Republican (Right) Viewpoints:

In Support of Holding Leaders Accountable for Inciting Violence or Undermining Democracy: A minority within the conservative camp might agree with this perspective, particularly those who are concerned about the long-term health of democratic institutions and the potential dangers of unchecked rhetoric. Estimated percentage: 20%.

In Support of Protecting Freedom of Expression for Political Leaders: The dominant view among conservatives likely centers on upholding traditional democratic values like free speech. This group believes that the electorate should be the ultimate judge of a leader's actions. Estimated percentage: 80%.

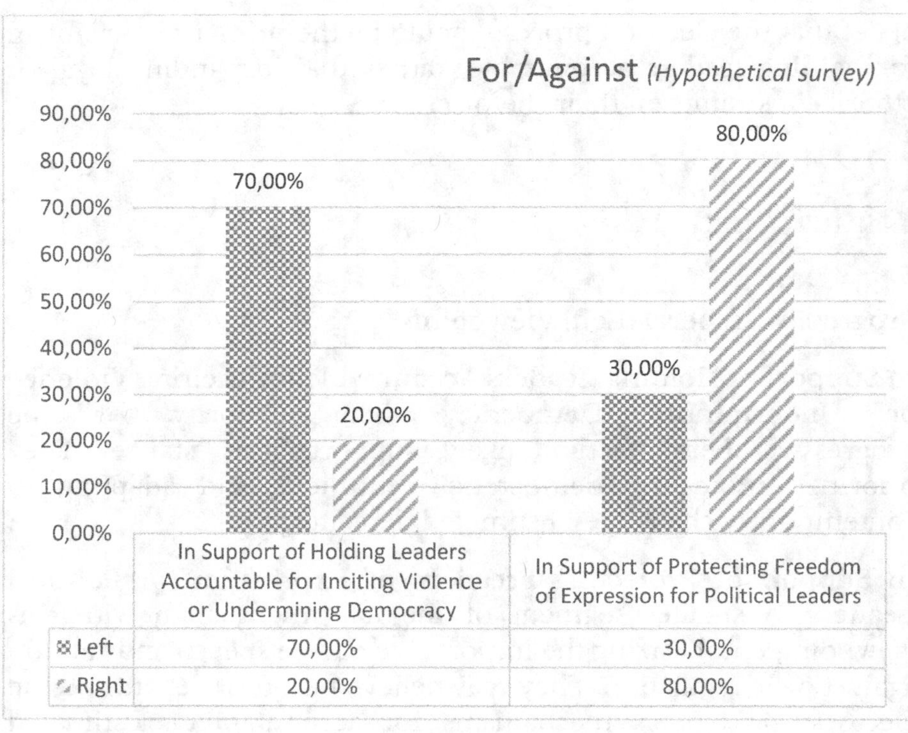

For/Against *(Hypothetical survey)*

	In Support of Holding Leaders Accountable for Inciting Violence or Undermining Democracy	In Support of Protecting Freedom of Expression for Political Leaders
Left	70,00%	30,00%
Right	20,00%	80,00%

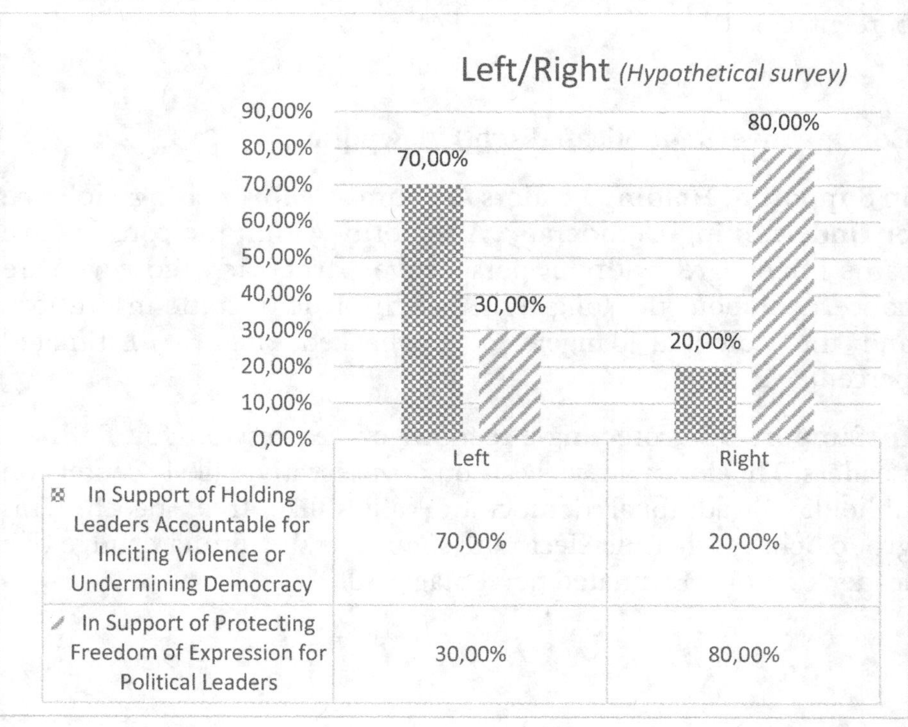

Left/Right *(Hypothetical survey)*

	Left	Right
In Support of Holding Leaders Accountable for Inciting Violence or Undermining Democracy	70,00%	20,00%
In Support of Protecting Freedom of Expression for Political Leaders	30,00%	80,00%

Motions of the debate

Coalition's Motion (Progressive Viewpoint):

"This house supports the enforcement of stricter accountability measures for political leaders whose rhetoric incites violence or undermines democratic processes."

Opposition's Motion (Conservative Viewpoint):

"This house opposes the imposition of additional restrictions on the freedom of expression of political leaders, upholding the principle that the electorate should judge their actions."

Coalition Speech

Ladies and gentlemen, esteemed judges, and fellow debaters, today we stand at a pivotal moment in the preservation of our democratic ideals. At the heart of this debate is a fundamental question: Should we, as a society, allow the unchecked rhetoric of political leaders to undermine the very fabric of our democracy?

Let us begin by acknowledging the sanctity of democratic institutions, the bulwarks of our freedom and equality. These institutions are not just abstract concepts; they are the embodiment of our rights, our freedoms, and our collective will. Yet, they stand threatened when leaders use their influential platforms to incite violence or erode democratic processes. History is replete with examples where demagoguery led to the disintegration of democratic systems. We need not look far into the past to find chilling instances where political rhetoric ignited the flames of division and violence.

But this debate is not just about the past; it is about our present and our future. In our own times, we have witnessed a disturbing rise in hate crimes following speeches that target specific groups. These are not mere coincidences. They are direct consequences of irresponsible rhetoric, echoing from the highest echelons of power to the streets of our cities. When leaders speak, their words carry weight, and with that weight comes responsibility.

Now, let's consider the role of leadership in shaping society. Leaders are not just political figures; they are role models, setting the moral compass for future generations. In every profession where the stakes are high – be it in law, medicine, or education – we demand accountability. Why should our political leaders be exempt? Setting higher standards for public figures fosters a culture of responsibility and integrity. It encourages thoughtful, constructive discourse, steering us away from the precipice of divisive and harmful politics.

In closing, I ask you to envision a world where our leaders are accountable for their words and actions, where our democratic institutions are robust and respected, and where our society is safe from the rhetoric of hate and division. This is not just an ideal; it is a necessity for the survival of our democracy. By supporting this motion, we take a stand for responsible leadership, for the protection of our democratic values, and for the future of our society. Let us choose a path that leads to unity, respect, and progress. Thank you.

Summary of the coalition's arguments

I. Protection of Democratic Institutions
A. Preventing the Erosion of Democratic Norms
- Incendiary rhetoric from leaders can undermine public trust in democratic processes.
- Historical examples show how demagoguery has led to the breakdown of democratic institutions.
B. Safeguarding Against Violence and Unrest
- There is a correlation between inflammatory political rhetoric and incidents of political violence.
- Cases where political speeches have directly inspired violent acts, demonstrating the real-world impact of irresponsible rhetoric.
II. Maintaining Social Harmony and Public Safety
A. Reducing Societal Division and Hatred
- Politically charged rhetoric often exacerbates social divisions and hatred.
- Studies indicate a rise in hate crimes following speeches that target specific groups.
B. Preventing the Spread of Misinformation

- Leaders' statements have a significant impact on public opinion and can spread misinformation.
- Instances where false claims by political figures have led to public harm or panic.
III. Upholding Responsible Leadership and Accountability
A. Setting Higher Standards for Public Figures
- Leaders should be role models, adhering to higher ethical and moral standards.
- Comparisons with other professions where accountability is strictly enforced (e.g., legal, medical fields).
B. Encouraging Thoughtful and Constructive Discourse
- Promoting accountability leads to more responsible and constructive political discourse.
- Examples of political environments with high standards leading to more productive and less divisive politics.

Opposition Speech

Ladies and gentlemen, esteemed panel, and fellow debaters, today I stand before you to champion a principle fundamental to the very essence of democracy: the freedom of expression. This hallowed right, enshrined in our constitutions and cherished in our hearts, is under siege by the motion presented today.

Let us embark on this journey of discourse by first recognizing that freedom of speech is not a mere luxury, but the bedrock of a free and open society. It is the right that guards all other rights. History teaches us valuable lessons – when the voices of leaders are stifled, society steps onto a slippery slope towards authoritarianism. Can we afford to forget how the suppression of political speech has, time and again, paved the way for tyrants and dictators?

Now, consider the pivotal role of the electorate in a democracy. It is the voters, the common people, who are the ultimate arbiters of political discourse. By suggesting that we need additional measures to hold leaders accountable, are we not undermining the intelligence and judgment of our citizens? The ballot box is the most powerful tool in a democracy, and it is there that leaders should, and are, held accountable.

Furthermore, the over-regulation of political speech risks creating an environment of censorship and subjectivity. Who decides what constitutes harmful rhetoric? Who draws the line between passionate debate and incitement? History is littered with instances where laws meant to protect, were used to suppress. We must be vigilant, for the road to censorship is often paved with good intentions.

In closing, I urge you to consider the implications of supporting this motion. Do we wish to tread a path that might lead to the erosion of our most fundamental freedom? Or do we choose to stand firm on the principles of liberty and free speech, trusting in the wisdom of our electorate and the resilience of our democratic institutions? The choice is clear. Let us oppose this motion and reaffirm our commitment to freedom, to democracy, and to the enduring power of the people's voice. Thank you.

Summary of the opposition's arguments

I. Preservation of Freedom of Expression
A. Fundamental Democratic Right
- Freedom of speech is a cornerstone of democratic societies, enshrined in many constitutions.
- Historical instances where curbing political speech led to authoritarianism.
B. Risk of Censorship and Subjectivity
- Imposing restrictions can lead to subjective interpretations of what constitutes harmful rhetoric.
- Examples of governments using similar laws to suppress dissent and control political narrative.
II. Role of the Electorate in Democracy
A. Voters as Ultimate Judges
- In a democracy, voters should assess and respond to political rhetoric, not legal or regulatory bodies.
- Instances where the electorate effectively held leaders accountable through the ballot box.
B. Dangers of Over-Regulation
- Excessive regulation of political speech can lead to an overly sanitized and unrepresentative political dialogue.

- Case studies showing how over-regulation led to a disconnect between political leaders and the public.
III. Impact on Political Discourse and Diversity of Opinion
A. Encouraging Open and Robust Debate
- Free political expression allows for a diversity of opinions and vigorous public debate, essential for a healthy democracy.
- Historical examples where open debate led to significant social and political progress.
B. Avoiding the Slippery Slope of Overreach
- Setting precedents for restricting political speech could lead to broader limitations on free expression.
- Examples where initial mild restrictions eventually led to widespread control over public discourse.

10 questions from the coalition to the opposition:

1. How would you address instances where political leaders' rhetoric has directly led to acts of violence or the breakdown of democratic processes?

2. What measures would you propose to ensure that the freedom of expression does not become a shield for spreading misinformation or hate speech?

3. In your view, is there a line where political rhetoric becomes harmful to society, and if so, how do you propose it be identified without regulation?

4. How can we rely solely on the electoral process for accountability when the effects of harmful rhetoric may be immediate and the electoral response is typically delayed?

5. Can you provide examples where unrestricted political speech has led to positive outcomes in situations of heightened social and political tension?

6. How does your stance account for the influence of digital platforms where political rhetoric can spread rapidly and incite immediate reactions?

7. Given the global rise in political polarization, how do you ensure that protecting freedom of speech does not exacerbate this division?

8. How do you propose to balance the rights of individuals or groups who may be adversely affected by political leaders' irresponsible speech with the leaders' right to free expression?

9. In cases where political speech has endangered public safety, how do you justify prioritizing the speaker's freedom over the safety of the populace?

10. How do you respond to the argument that with great power comes greater responsibility, and thus political leaders should be held to higher standards of speech?

10 questions from the opposition to the coalition:

1. How do you propose to define and measure 'incitement to violence' or 'undermining democracy' in a way that is objective and non-partisan?

2. What safeguards would you suggest to ensure that increased accountability does not lead to censorship or the suppression of legitimate political discourse?

3. How can you guarantee that the enforcement of stricter accountability measures will not be used as a political tool against opposition voices?

4. Can you provide historical examples where similar measures to hold leaders accountable have led to improved democratic processes without impinging on free speech?

5. How would you address the concern that imposing restrictions on political leaders' speech might set a precedent for limiting the free speech of citizens?

6. In your view, how does one balance the need for accountability with the risk of creating a chilling effect on political expression and innovation?

7. How would your proposed measures deal with the subjective nature of interpreting what constitutes harmful rhetoric versus passionate political speech?

8. What mechanisms would you suggest to ensure that these accountability measures are applied equally across the political spectrum, without bias?

9. How do you respond to the argument that the electorate, not regulatory bodies, should be the judge of a political leader's rhetoric?

10. Can you illustrate how your proposed accountability measures would be implemented in a diverse and pluralistic society without infringing on cultural or individual expressions?

Potential solutions to reconcile the two parties

In the quest for a harmonious balance between freedom of expression and accountability in political discourse, there emerges a pathway paved with mutual understanding and compromise. One potential solution lies in **establishing clear guidelines** for political speech, defined collaboratively by representatives from various political spectrums, ensuring objectivity and non-partisanship. These guidelines would not be rigid laws but rather a moral compass to guide political leaders, respecting the essence of free speech while promoting responsible rhetoric.

Building on this foundation, a system of **voluntary compliance** could be established where political parties and leaders commit to these guidelines, demonstrating their dedication to upholding democratic values. This approach respects the autonomy of political figures while encouraging a culture of accountability.

To address concerns about subjective interpretations of harmful rhetoric, an **independent advisory council** could be established. This council, comprising members from diverse political and social backgrounds, would offer non-binding recommendations in cases of disputed political speech. Their role would not be to penalize but to provide a balanced perspective, respecting the opposition's concern about potential censorship.

Understanding the power of rhetoric, especially in the digital age, both sides might agree on the importance of **media literacy programs**. These programs, aimed at the public, especially the youth, would educate citizens on discerning political rhetoric, understanding persuasive techniques, and recognizing misinformation. Such initiatives empower the electorate, a key point for the opposition, to make informed decisions without infringing upon the freedom of political speech.

Another conciliatory approach could be the **promotion of public forums** for open debate. These forums, held regularly and accessible to all, would allow political leaders to express their views openly and engage with the public and critics alike, fostering a culture of transparency and direct accountability.

Recognizing the role of digital platforms in shaping public opinion, a collaborative effort could be made to **work with social media companies** in flagging content that is blatantly misleading or incendiary, without removing it. This approach respects the right to free speech while addressing the coalition's concern about the spread of harmful misinformation.

In instances where political speech is linked to violence or unrest, both sides might find common ground in supporting **reparative and community-focused initiatives** led by the involved political parties or leaders. This would not be an admission of guilt, but rather a constructive way to heal and address any societal divisions that might have arisen, aligning with the coalition's focus on maintaining social harmony.

To ensure ongoing dialogue and adaptation of these solutions, the establishment of an **annual review board** could be agreed upon. This board would assess the effectiveness of the implemented measures and make adjustments as necessary, keeping pace with the evolving political and social landscape.

In extreme cases where political rhetoric poses a clear and immediate threat to public safety or democratic institutions, a **bipartisan emergency council** could be convened to assess the situation and offer guidance. This would be a rare and last resort measure, reflecting the gravity of such situations while acknowledging the opposition's concerns about over-regulation.

Finally, both sides might agree on the value of **civic education programs** that emphasize the responsibilities of political leaders and the rights of citizens. These programs would aim to foster a politically engaged and informed electorate, capable of holding leaders accountable through informed voting, a principle dearly held by the opposition.

Through these measures, a delicate balance can be struck, one that upholds the sanctity of free speech while ensuring that political discourse remains a tool for democracy, not a weapon against it.

Recommended Resources

On Liberty[45] by John Stuart Mill

Coalition/Opposition Breakdown: 40/60

This book leans more towards the opposition's viewpoint as it is a seminal work advocating for the importance of freedom of speech and individual liberty. Mill argues against censorship and emphasizes the value of allowing all ideas to be expressed, even those that are unpopular, for the betterment of society. While it does touch on the responsibilities that come with freedom, its primary focus is on defending the liberty of expression.

How to Cure A Fanatic[46] by Amos Oz

Coalition/Opposition Breakdown: 50/50

This book offers a balanced view, addressing the dangers of fanaticism (aligning with the coalition's concerns about harmful rhetoric) while also highlighting the importance of dialogue and

---

[45] https://amzn.to/3RIrYkY
[46] https://amzn.to/41qJeyA

understanding (echoing the opposition's emphasis on freedom of speech). Oz's perspective on using humor and empathy to counteract fanaticism provides insights relevant to both sides of the debate.

Defending My Enemy: American Nazis, the Skokie Case, and the Risks of Freedom[47] by Aryeh Neier

Coalition/Opposition Breakdown: 30/70

This book supports the opposition's stance to a greater extent, detailing a case where the rights of a Nazi group to march in Skokie, Illinois, were defended despite the potential for inflammatory and harmful rhetoric. It emphasizes the importance of protecting freedom of speech, even for the most detestable viewpoints, underscoring a key argument of the opposition.

Giving Offense: Essays on Censorship[48] by J. M. Coetzee

Coalition/Opposition Breakdown: 45/55

Coetzee's collection of essays slightly favors the opposition's viewpoint. It delves into the complexities of censorship, exploring its consequences and the often-subjective nature of what is considered offensive. While it acknowledges the potential harm of certain speech, the primary focus is on the risks and ethical concerns associated with censorship.

The Master Switch: The Rise and Fall of Information Empires[49] by Tim Wu

Coalition/Opposition Breakdown: 50/50

This book provides a nuanced view that intersects with both sides of the debate. It examines the history and future of information

---

[47] https://amzn.to/3RgneBG
[48] https://amzn.to/48jrgQM
[49] https://amzn.to/4aiV7KS

technologies and how control over these can impact freedom of speech and democracy. Wu's analysis of the balance between free expression and the regulation of information platforms touches on concerns of both the coalition and the opposition.

Conclusion

As we conclude our journey, we are left with a profound understanding of the complexities and vulnerabilities of modern democracies. This book has not only highlighted the challenges and divisions we face but also illuminated the resilience and adaptability inherent in democratic systems.

In these pages, we have traversed the landscape of political loyalty versus constitutional duty, witnessing the tug-of-war between personal beliefs and public responsibilities. We have seen how the media, both a tool for enlightenment and a weapon of misinformation, plays a crucial role in shaping political narratives. The legitimacy of election outcomes and the delicate balance of power between the executive and legislative branches have been scrutinized, reminding us of the fragility of the systems we often take for granted.

As we reflect on the journey, it's important to remember that democracy, at its core, is an ever-evolving process, not a static entity. It is a system built on the principles of dialogue, dissent, and diversity. The challenges it faces today, from polarization to misinformation, are tests of its resilience and capacity for reform and innovation. The emotional fatigue and frustration we observe in the political landscape are not just symptoms of a system in distress but also signals for the need for active engagement and constructive dialogue.

The future of democracy is not predetermined. It is shaped by the actions, choices, and voices of its constituents. This book serves as a call to action for all who engage with it - to participate, to debate, to question, and to listen. It is a reminder that the strength of a democracy lies not just in its institutions, but in the engagement and will of its people.

As we close this book, let us not see it as an end, but as a beginning - a starting point for deeper engagement, understanding, and commitment to the principles of democracy. May the insights gained from these pages inspire us to be active participants in the continuous shaping of our democratic landscape, fostering a society that is more inclusive, just, and resilient.

In the end, "Democracy on the Edge" is more than just an analysis of the current state of democracies; it is a testament to the enduring spirit of democratic ideals and a guide for navigating the challenges that lie ahead. The future of democracy depends on our collective effort to uphold its values and adapt to an ever-changing world.

Index

Books in this series

"Society in Debate™" is a groundbreaking series that delves into the heart of contemporary issues shaping our world. Each volume in this series is dedicated to exploring critical topics that spark passionate discussions and debates across various spheres of society. What sets this series apart is its unique format, a format that brings to life the dynamic and often polarized viewpoints that characterize modern discourse.

At the core of each book in the "Society in Debate™" series is the commitment to presenting arguments from two opposing camps. This approach mirrors the real-world complexity of these issues, where seldom is there a clear-cut right or wrong answer. Readers are invited to explore structured and well-articulated speeches that represent each side of the debate, offering a comprehensive understanding of the arguments and counterarguments.

To further enhance the reader's engagement, each volume includes a series of challenging questions posed by each side. These questions are designed to provoke thought, encourage critical analysis, and allow readers to immerse themselves more deeply in the intricacies of the debates. They serve as a catalyst for reflection, pushing readers to consider their own viewpoints and perhaps even reevaluate their stances on key issues.

Moreover, recognizing the importance of finding common ground, each book in the series explores potential avenues for reconciliation and compromise. This feature is essential, as it acknowledges the complexity of societal debates and the need for solutions that can bridge divided opinions. By presenting these potential solutions, the series underscores the possibility of progress and understanding, even in the face of deep-seated disagreements.

To provide readers with comprehensive insight, each volume also offers a curated list of recommended resources. This feature is particularly valuable for readers who wish to explore the subjects in greater depth.

The "Society in Debate™" series is more than just a collection of books; it is a platform for understanding, discussion, and learning.

It invites readers to engage with some of the most pressing issues of our time, providing a space for contemplation and dialogue. As the series continues to grow, it remains committed to enriching public discourse and contributing to a more informed and thoughtful society.

<u>Already published:</u>

<u>Society in Debate: Perspectives on Key Issues</u> by Maggie White

Decriminalization of cannabis - Climate change – Abortion – Immigration - Free speech - Universal basic income - Artificial intelligence - Capital punishment - Internet regulation - Gun control

<u>Society in Debate Vol. 2: Perspectives on Key Issues</u> by Maggie White

Animal Rights - Genetic Engineering - Nuclear Energy - Universal Healthcare - Mandatory vaccination - Cultural appropriation - Capitalism vs. socialism - Age restrictions for voting and other activities - Electoral College - The use of military force and intervention in foreign affairs

<u>Debates on Landmarks & Monuments: A Multifaceted Exploration</u> by Catherine E. Marlowe (Society in Debate Vol. 3)

Preservation vs. Modernization - Cultural Appropriation in Monument Design - Monuments Reflecting Controversial Historical Figures - Impact of Tourism on Landmarks - Representation in Monuments - Economic Cost vs. Cultural Value of Landmarks - Landmarks as Symbols of National Identity - Environmental Impact of Building and Maintaining Landmarks - Public Accessibility vs. Preservation - Digital Reconstruction of Lost Monuments

<u>Modern Faith, Ancient Walls: Navigating the Future of Religious Buildings</u> by Ethan Hawthorne (Society in Debate Vol. 4)

Use of Public Funds - Secular Usage of Religious Spaces - Architectural Dominance in Cityscapes - Representation of Diverse Religions - Sustainable Architecture in Religious Buildings - Modernization vs. Preservation - Commercialization and Tourism - Inclusive vs. Exclusive Architectural Design - Impact of Technology on Religious Architecture - Cultural Appropriation in Architectural Styles